NEEDLEPOINT DESIGNS

Cushions · Pictures · Covers

Also by Julie Hasler

WILD FLOWERS IN CROSS-STITCH

(Blandford, 1989)

DOGS AND PUPPIES IN CROSS-STITCH

(Blandford, 1989)

NEEDLEPOINT

DESIGNS
Cushions · Pictures · Covers

JULIE HASLER

BLANDFORD

This book is dedicated to Steve Matthews
for all his love and support

A BLANDFORD BOOK

First published in the UK 1991
by Blandford
Villiers House
41/47 Strand
London
WC2N 5JE

Distributed in the United States
by Sterling Publishing Co., Inc.
387 Park Avenue South, New York, NY 10016-8810

Distributed in Australia
by Capricorn Link (Australia) Pty Ltd
P.O. Box 665, Lane Cove, NSW 2066

British Library Cataloguing in Publication Data

Hasler, Julie
  Needlepoint Designs.
  1. Embroidery canvas, designs.
  I. Title
  746.442

  ISBN 0-7137-2169-3

Typeset by Litho Link Limited, Welshpool, Powys, Wales
Printed and bound in Singapore by Kyodo Printing Co Pte Ltd

Contents

Acknowledgements

My special thanks go to all my loyal homeworkers who helped me with this book, stitching the designs and making up the cushions: Louise Wells, Odette Robinson, Elaine Bloomfield, Christine Gorton, Beryl Garlick, Caroline Hughes, Ella Birch and Libby. My thanks to Cara Ackerman, from Dunlicraft, for supplying the canvas and wools for this book, and H. W. Peel & Co. Ltd for the graph paper.

Introduction

This book adds something new, fresh and extremely stylish to the needlepoint repertoire. It introduces the method of working directly from a charted design onto an unmarked canvas.

Contained in the book is a wide variety of designs – 46 in all – with something to appeal to everyone, whatever their taste. There are picture cushion covers (which can also be used as framed pictures), geometric patterns, floral patterns, traditional and modern designs. Most of the designs can be adapted to other uses, e.g. as chair seats or church kneelers.

The large-scale charts are very easy to follow, and colour keys are given for all designs, although these are just a guideline. You can incorporate your own colours to suit your décor if you prefer. Clear instructions and diagrams take you through making your cushions from start to finish, enabling both the experienced and inexperienced worker to complete these lovely designs.

Happy stitching!

Materials required

Needlepoint is a fairly inexpensive hobby, requiring only a few basic materials.

FRAME

It would be an advantage if you worked your design on a frame, thus preventing it from pulling out of shape and having to be stretched when completed. The other advantage of using a frame is that the canvas is held at a permanent tension, thus making the stitching even and easier to work.

As your finished cushion cover design will measure 14 × 14 in (36 × 36 cm), an 18 in (45 cm) or 22 in (55 cm) hand-held frame would be ideal. These are available from most large department stores or craft shops.

CANVAS

There are two distinct types of needlepoint canvas: single-mesh (mono canvas) and double-mesh (duo canvas) both of which are available in many mesh sizes. As is usual for cushion covers, all the designs in this book have been calculated for use with double-mesh canvas, the size being 10 mesh per inch (10 stitches per inch). Make sure you obtain the correct mesh size, otherwise your cushion will end up a different finished size.

NEEDLES

You will need to use a blunt tapestry needle with a rounded tip and an elongated eye. Ensure that the needle clears the hole of the canvas without spreading the threads. For 10 mesh per inch canvas, you will find that a No. 18 needle works best.

YARNS

All the designs in this book are keyed to DMC tapestry wool, a superior quality non-divisible 4-ply wool which is ideal for needlepoint, being both mothproof and colourfast. It is wonderful to work with and is available in 430 different colours and shades. DMC tapestry wool is widely available in large department stores and craft shops.

BACKING FABRIC

You will need a strong backing fabric to finish off your cushion. Velvet, dralon, or any other medium-to-heavy weight fabric will suffice. Curtain material is good, and you can often find this in remnant boxes.

CUSHION PAD

A 14 × 14 in (36 × 36 cm) square fibre-filled or feather-filled cushion pad completes your list of materials. You can easily make your own cushion pads using calico, and filling with kapok or something similar, such as all-purpose filling.

Important advice

FOLLOWING A CHART

All the designs in this book are shown in chart form. The charts are very easy to follow, so don't worry if you are a beginner. Each square on the chart represents one needlepoint stitch to be taken on the canvas, and each different symbol represents a different colour. See how simple it is?

PREPARING YOUR CANVAS

First, cut your canvas to size. For each cushion, you will need a piece of canvas measuring approximately 2–2½ in (5–6 cm) larger than your finished design, i.e. 16–16½ in (40.5–41.5 cm) square.

If you decide not to work your design on a frame, you will probably find that the raw edges of the canvas will snag your clothing and damage the wool during sewing. To prevent this happening, you can bind the raw edges of the canvas either with masking tape or machine-stitched double fold bias binding.

WHERE TO BEGIN THE DESIGN

There are no hard and fast rules on where to begin sewing your design, it is really a matter of personal choice. Some prefer to start at the centre point and work out, or to complete the main motif and then fill the background as the last step. I like to begin at the bottom left-hand corner and work up row by row, but it is really up to you. Choose whatever you feel most comfortable doing.

If you wish to draw any guidelines onto your canvas, ensure that your marking medium is waterproof. Non-soluble inks and waterproof felt-tip pens both work well. If you are unsure, experiment on a piece of scrap canvas first.

THREADING THE NEEDLE

Special needle threaders are usually very flimsy and quickly get broken, but threading your needle can be made very simple by cutting a piece of paper about ½ in (1 cm) square, placing the end of your wool along the centre line of the square, then folding the paper in half around the wool and passing this through the eye of the needle. It is preferable to work with yarn no longer than 18 in (45 cm).

PROPER COVERAGE OF THE CANVAS

Remember that care must be taken to keep the stitches at an even tension. If the stitches are too tight, the canvas will show through and the needlepoint will become distorted.

TWISTED YARN

Your yarn may become twisted while working. If this happens, hold the needlepoint up and let both the needle and yarn hang down. The yarn will then untwist. Never continue working with twisted yarn as it will not give sufficient coverage of the canvas.

Stitching techniques

The designs in this book are worked in half-cross stitch (tent stitch). Half-cross stitch is always worked so that the stitches slant from left to right.

1. Begin at the top left-hand corner, bring the needle from the back to the front of the canvas (see arrow on Diagram 1), leaving approximately ¾–1 in (2–3 cm) of yarn at the back of the work. This will be sewn in when the first few stitches are made. *Never use knots.*

2. Push the needle into the next hole to the right and above the first and bring it back through the hole immediately below, as shown in Diagram 1.

3. Work rows straight from left to right. If worked correctly, the stitches will be straight on the wrong side of the canvas.

4. When working small areas, turn the canvas upside-down at the end of each row and proceed with the next row, or simply just work from right to left, as shown in Diagram 2.

5. The finishing threads should be worked in on the wrong side of your work, as shown in Diagram 3.

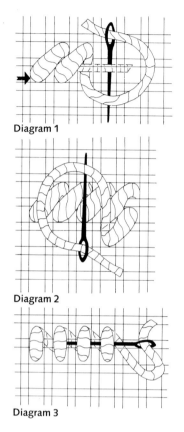

Diagram 1

Diagram 2

Diagram 3

Stretching

If you have not used a frame you will probably find that your finished design has pulled slightly out of shape and may require stretching before you make it into your cushion. This is very simple to do. With a piece of plywood, some rust-proof tacks and a large piece of blotting paper you are set up to do this at home.

Moisten a towel in cold water, and roll the needlepoint in the towel. Leave it in the towel overnight to ensure that both the canvas and the yarn are thoroughly and evenly dampened. Never saturate the canvas by holding it under the tap as that much water is not necessary.

Place the blotting paper onto the board and mark the desired finished size of the needlepoint (in this case 14 × 14 in (36 × 36 cm)) on the blotting paper, taking care that all four corners are straight. Stretch the canvas on the board with the right side facing the blotting paper, and place tacks in the margins about ½ in (1 cm) apart. It may take some pulling to get the needlepoint straight, but do not be afraid of this stress. Leave the canvas on the board, away from any direct sunlight and heat, until completely dry. If the needlepoint has been pulled badly out of shape, the stretching process may need to be repeated.

10

Making up your cushion

1 When your needlepoint design has been completed, trim the canvas leaving a margin of approximately 1 in (2.5 cm) of unworked canvas all the way around.

2 Place the needlepoint and backing fabric together, right sides facing, and machine stitch around three sides, stitching as close as possible to the worked area.

3 Snip off any excess canvas across the corners, press the seams open and turn the cushion to the right side.

4 Insert your cushion pad, and very neatly slipstitch the opening to close.

Your cushion is now complete!

Adapting your designs for use as chair seats

The classic designs shown in this book can be adapted for virtually any chair seat simply by adjusting the dimensions of the background area.

First establish the finished size you want to achieve. Remove the chair seat and measure it carefully, ensuring that you take the tape measure over the rounded surface down to the lower edges. Measure from the front to the back and along the front and back edges. Draw the outline of the embroidered area onto the canvas using a waterproof marking pen.

Next decide on the positioning of your motif, and mark the centre of the motif on the canvas. Mark the vertical centre line of the canvas, the horizontal centre line of the motif and the horizontal line of the canvas (which should be slightly above the centre of the motif). Bind the raw edges of the canvas and mount it on a frame. Work the design evenly. Before blocking the work, ensure that the embroidered area completely covers the chair pad. If it does not, simply add a few rows of stitches around the edges.

Remove the pad or seat from the chair, measure and mark the centre point on each side. Place the needlepoint embroidery right side down on a flat surface and lay the pad on top, upside down. Using drawing pins, fasten the needlepoint to the underside of the pad, close to the edge. Begin by fastening the centre points of each side. Continue by fastening all four corners, then insert the drawing pins along all four sides approximately ¾ in (2 cm) apart. Check frequently to ensure that the work is taut and straight, adjusting the pins if necessary. When you are satisfied that the work is positioned correctly and smoothly, fasten it permanently with upholstery tacks, removing the drawing pins as you go. Trim away any excess canvas. To neaten the underside of the pad, cut a piece of strong fabric slightly larger than the underside of the pad. Turn the edges under, press carefully, then slipstitch onto the edges of the canvas.

1

White
stallion

■	7715	pale grey	⧄ white
☐	7508	dark tan	‖ black

Photo on p.18

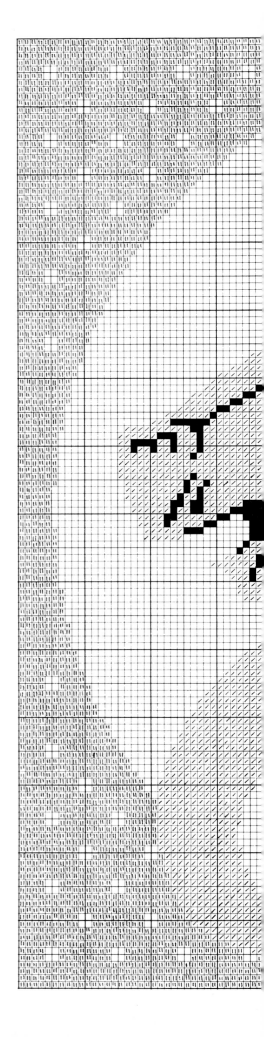

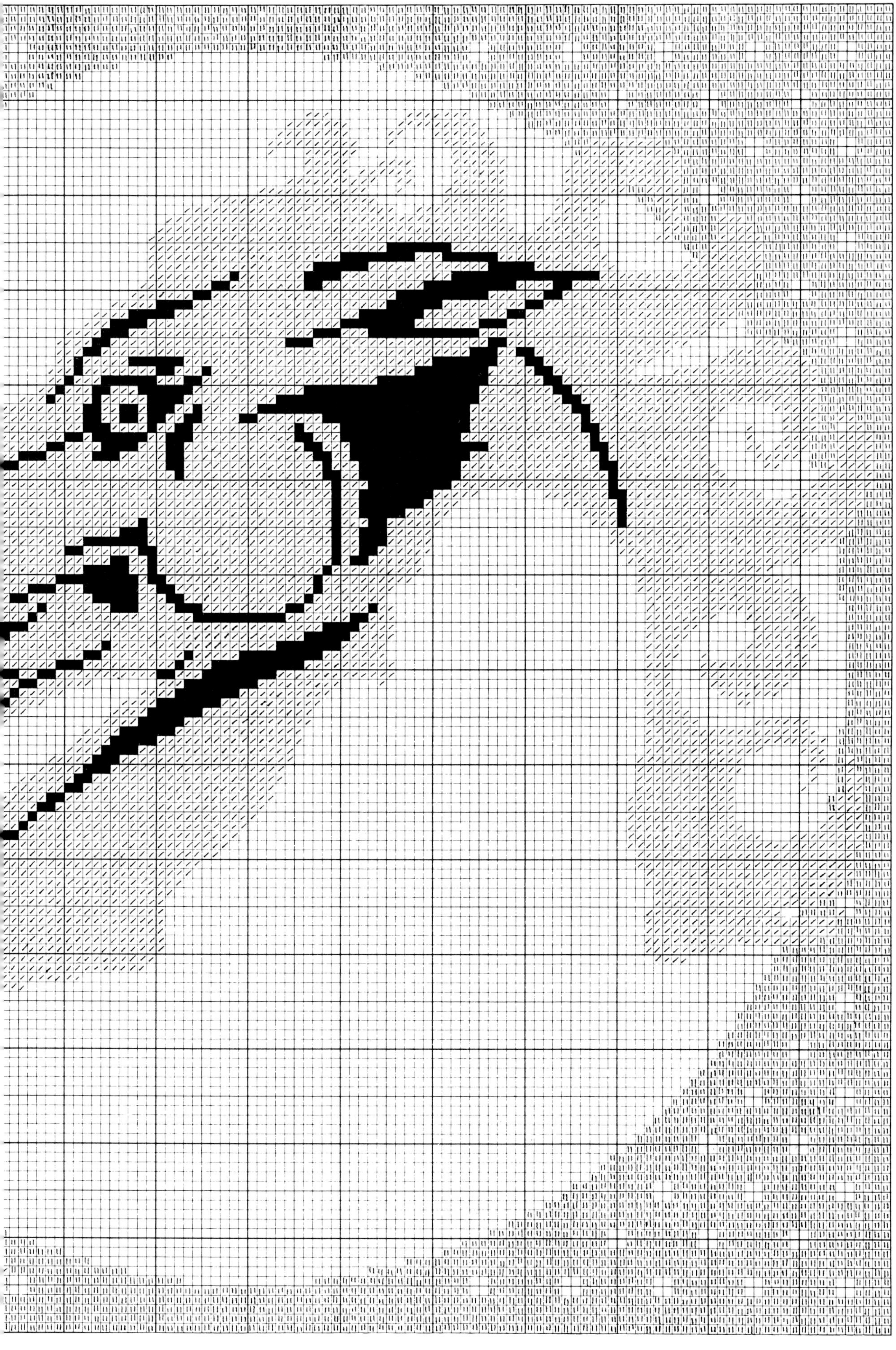

Spotted dog

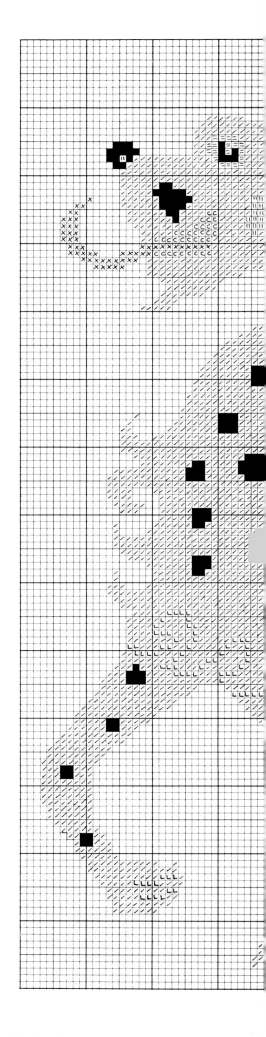

- ■ black
- □ 7138 dark red
- L 7715 pale grey
- ‖ 7618 medium grey
- ⊟ 7467 brown
- ⧄ white
- ✕ 7852 pink
- C 7622 dark grey

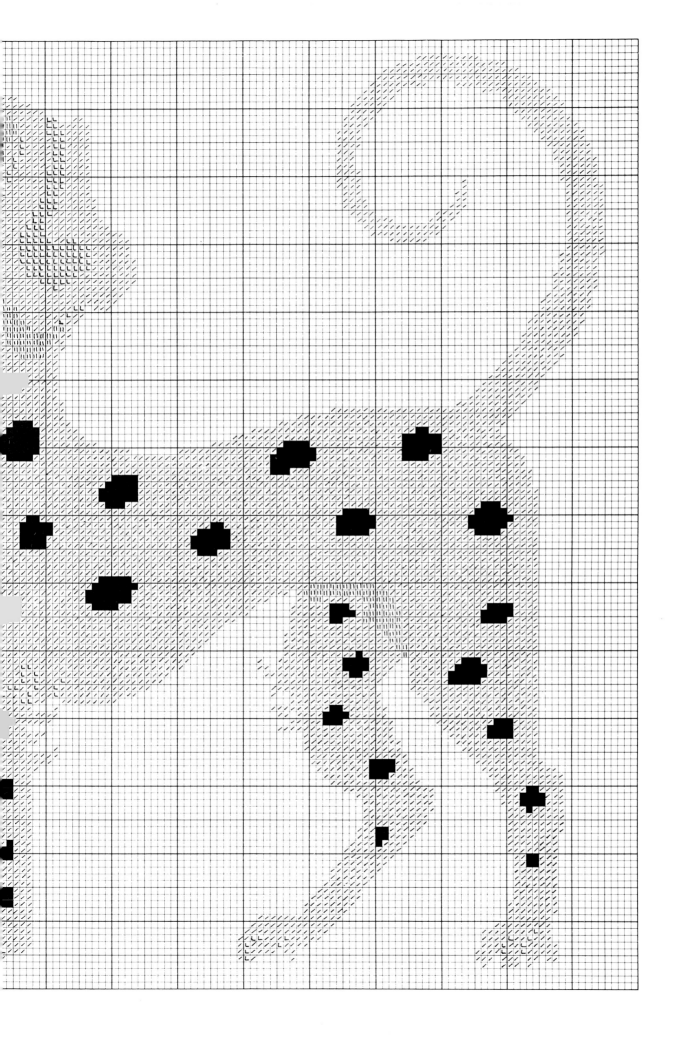

3

Winter snow scene

■ 7302 sky blue

□ 7389 dark green

⧄ 7121 pale flesh pink

◪ 7772 pale green

⨯ 7852 pink

⧅ 7321 pale grey/green

‖ 7870 grey/green

＝ 7766 dark tan

• 7715 pale grey

C white

○ 7394 khaki green

⫶ 7506 tan

Photo on p.18

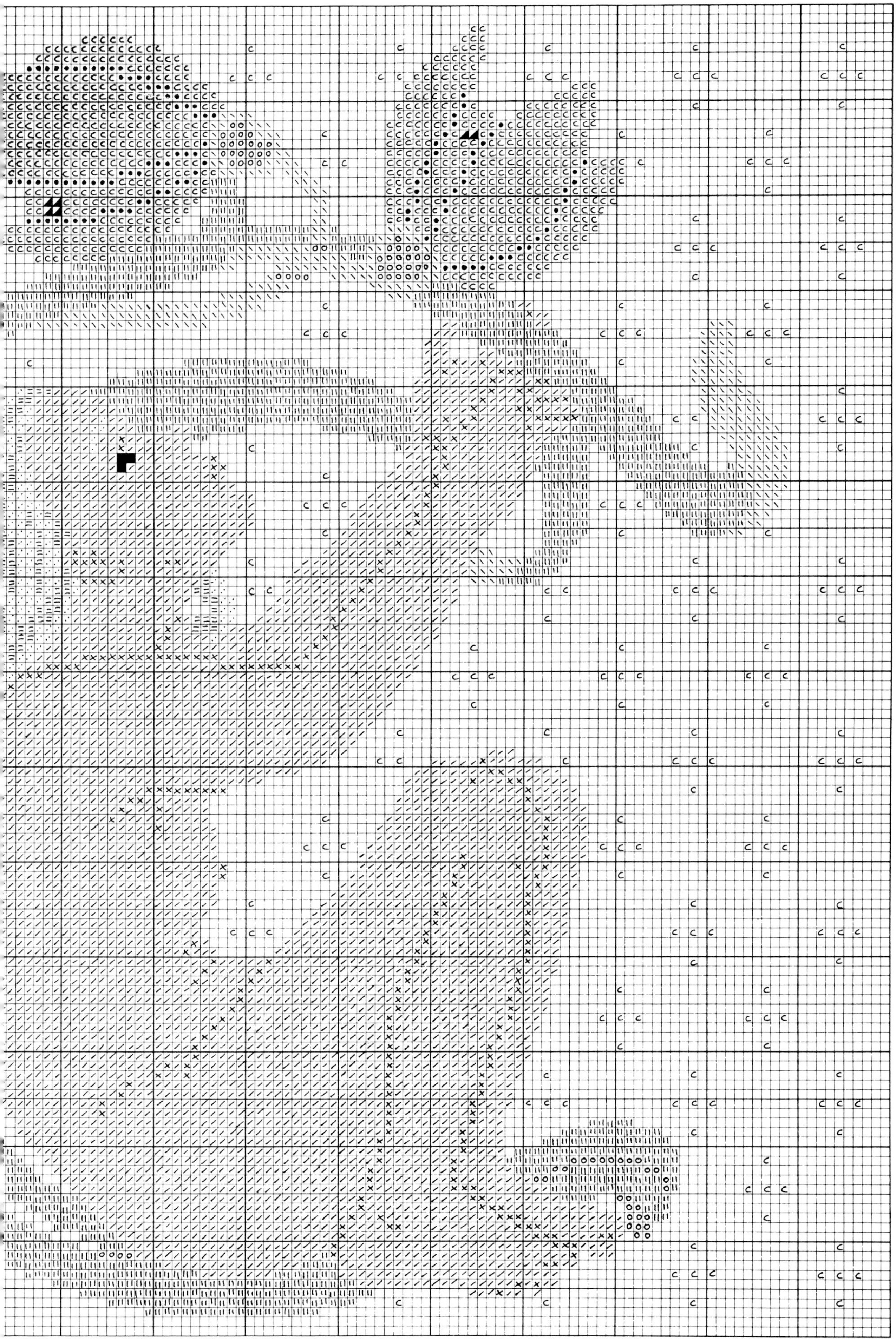

White stallion
See p.12

Winter snow scene
See p.16

Tiger
See p.20

Japanese lady
See p.22

Tiger

	black		7971 dark yellow
	7345 medium green		7437 orange
	7445 rust		7347 dark green

Photo on p.19

Japanese
lady

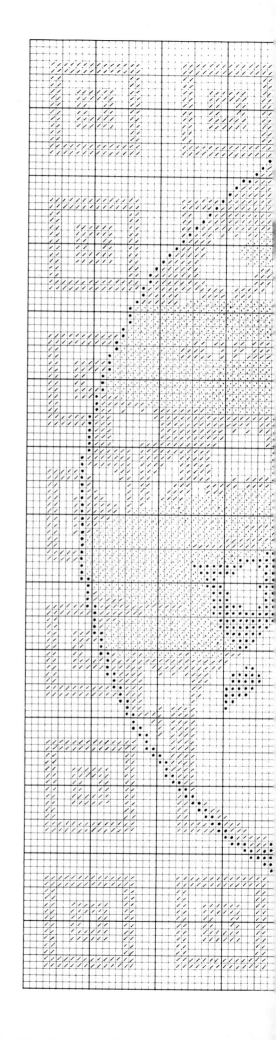

⊡ white   ☐ 7849 red

⊘ 7292 steel grey   ⊡ black

Photo on p.19

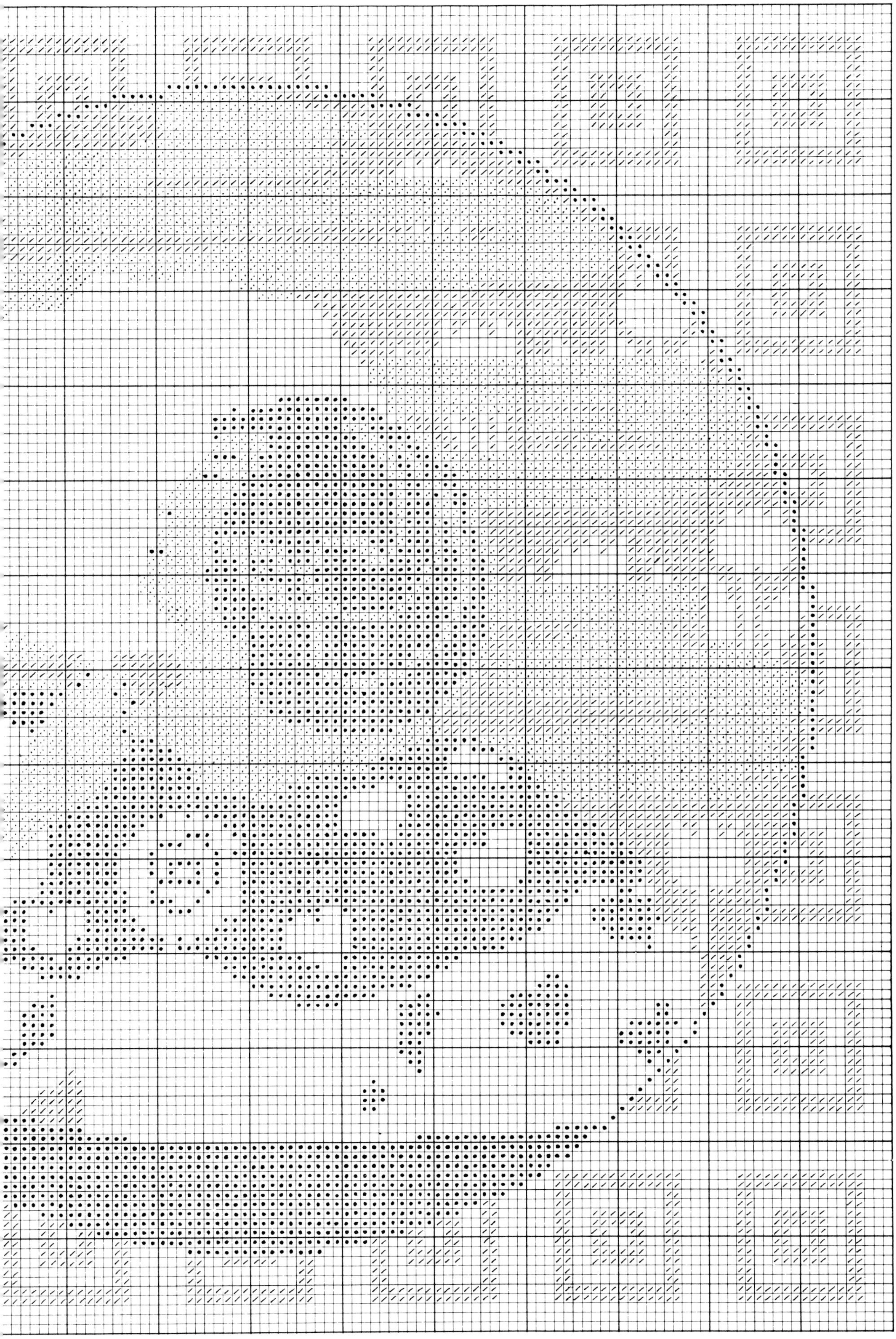

6

Elephant

■ 7727 pale yellow		7 white	
□ 7314 sky blue		☰ 7168 brown	
◪ black		Ⅰ 7828 pale blue	
◿ 7715 pale grey		─ 7245 mauve	
☒ 7285 medium grey		‖ 7911 green	
⊡ 7605 rose pink		C 7387 dark green	

Photo on p.26

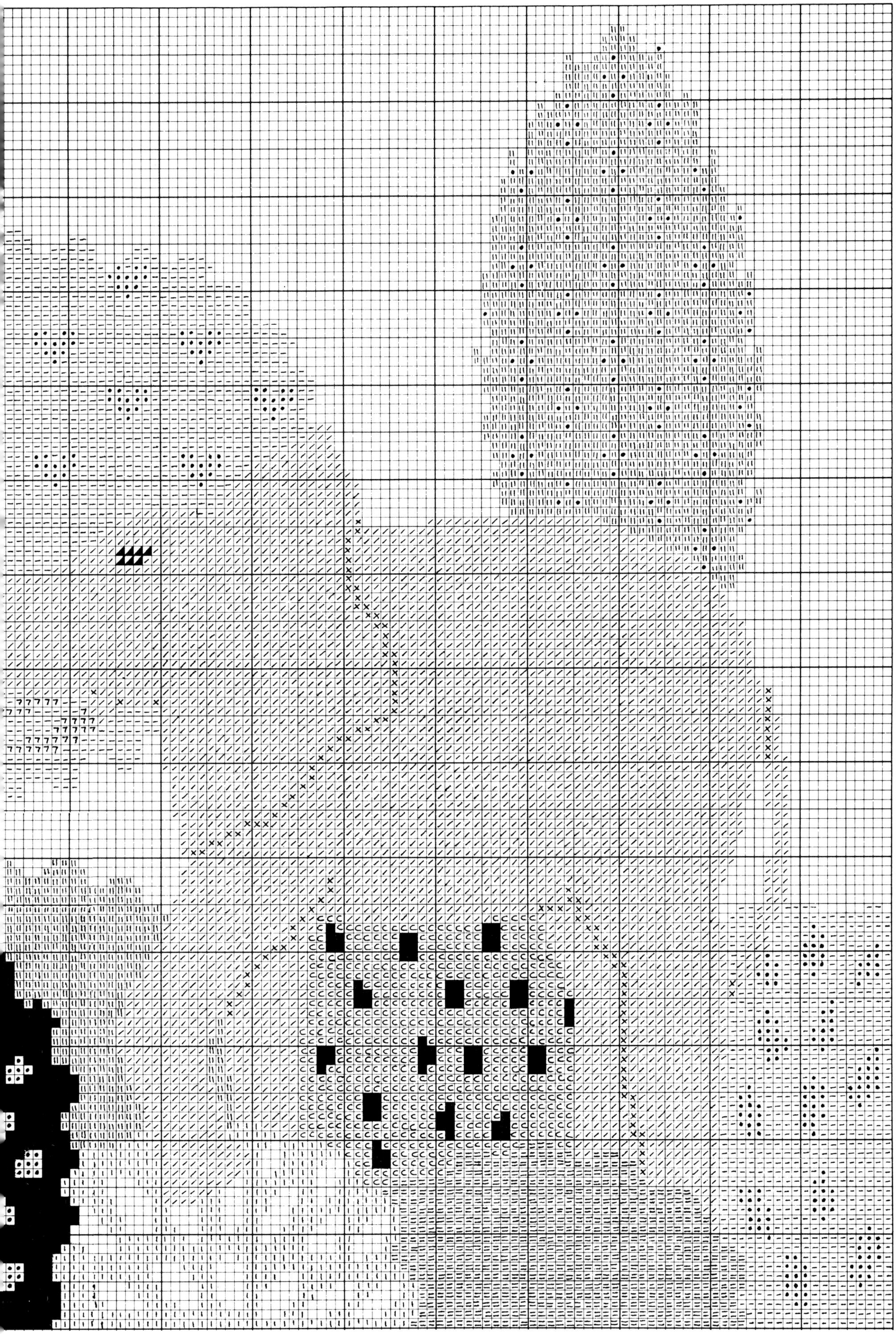

Elephant

See p.24

7

Egyptian picture (1)

	black		7598 electric blue
	7287 air force blue		7947 dark orange
	7861 turquoise		7496 brown
	white		7505 tan
	7360 rust		

Photo on p.30

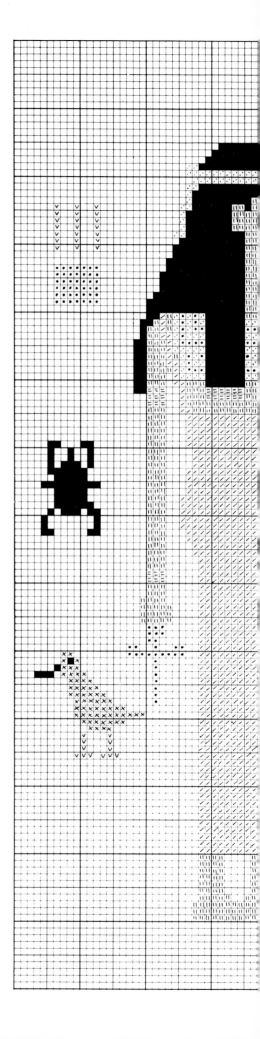

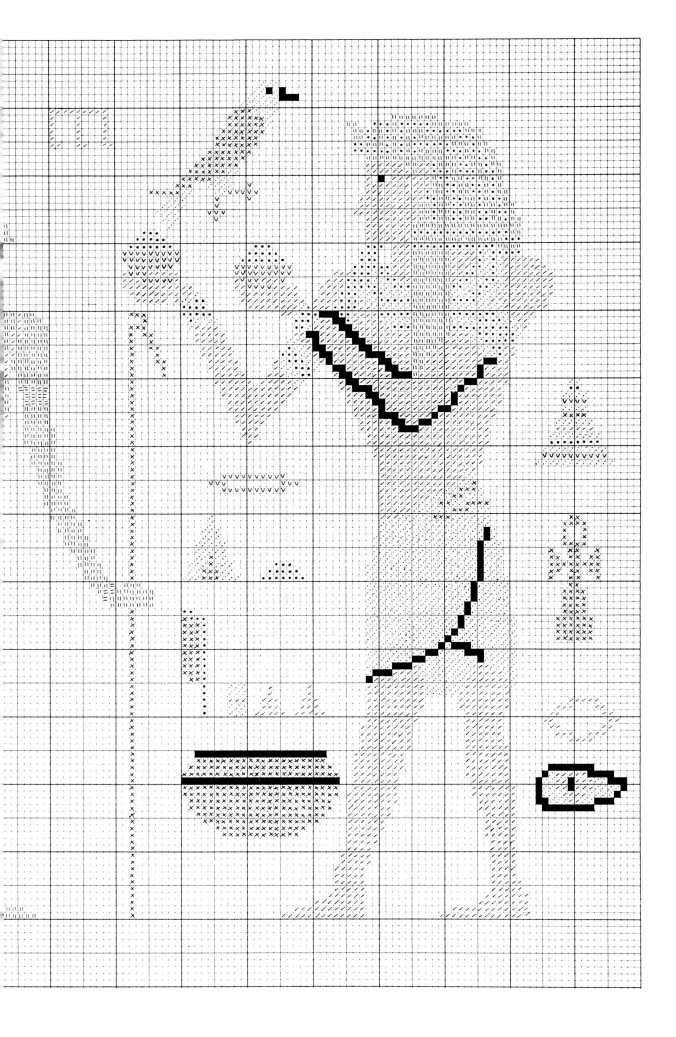

Egyptian picture (1)

See p.28

Egyptian picture (2)

See p.32

Egyptian picture (2)

■ black

⊡ 7215 dark flesh pink

▢ 7491 cream

◫ 7479 brown

◞ 7922 tan

◳ 7768 green

⧄ white

⊠ 7416 muddy brown

⧑ 7800 pale blue

ⓒ 7782 dark mustard

⊟ 7593 steel blue

Photo on p.31

9

Pastel
weave

•	7709 lilac	☒	7282 grey
╱	7727 pale yellow	◺	7954 pale turquoise
☐	7798 sky blue	‖	7102 pink

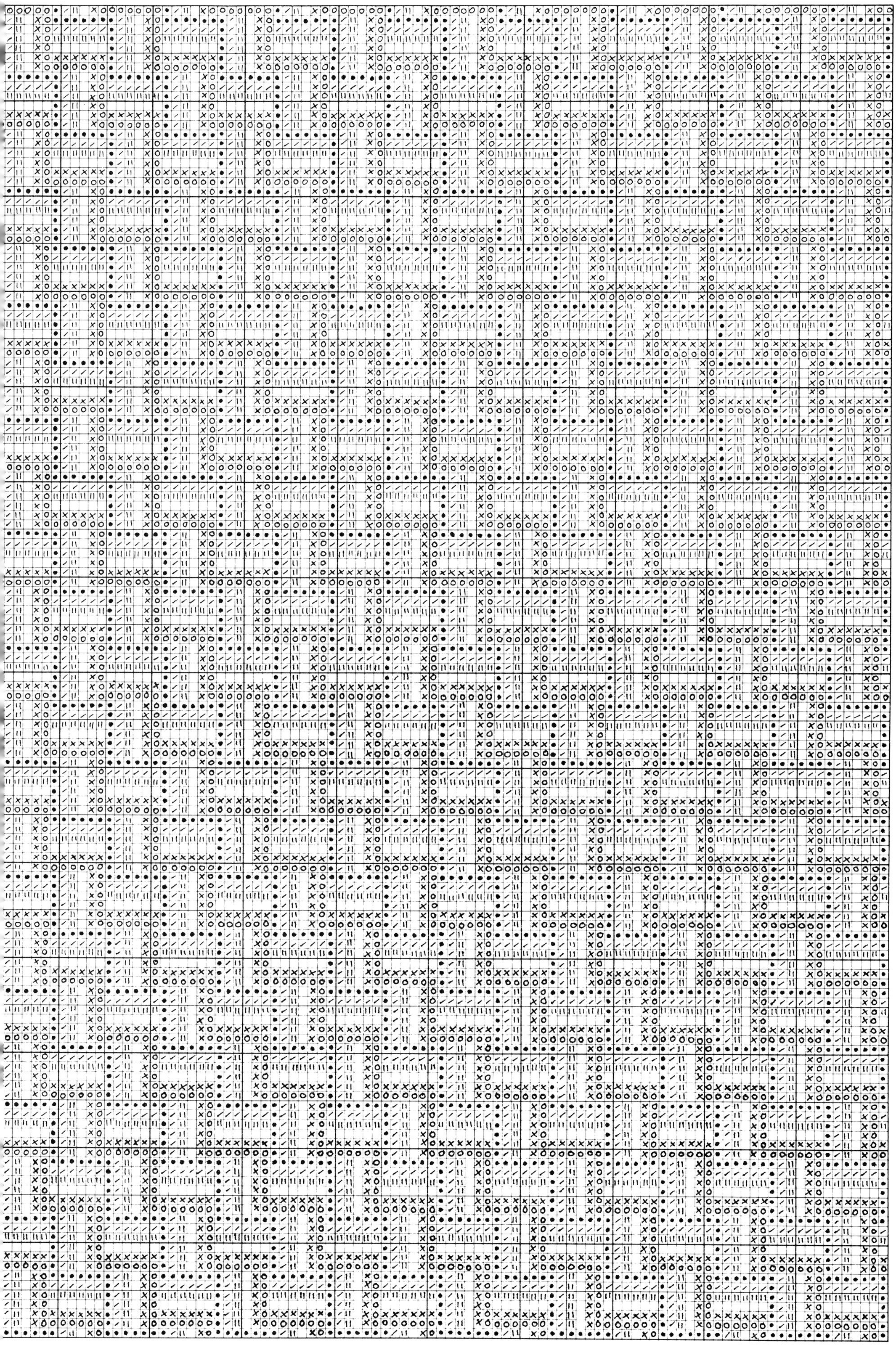

Pastel blocks

☑ 7799 sky blue   © 7727 pale yellow

☐ 7709 lilac   ⅠⅠ 7102 pink

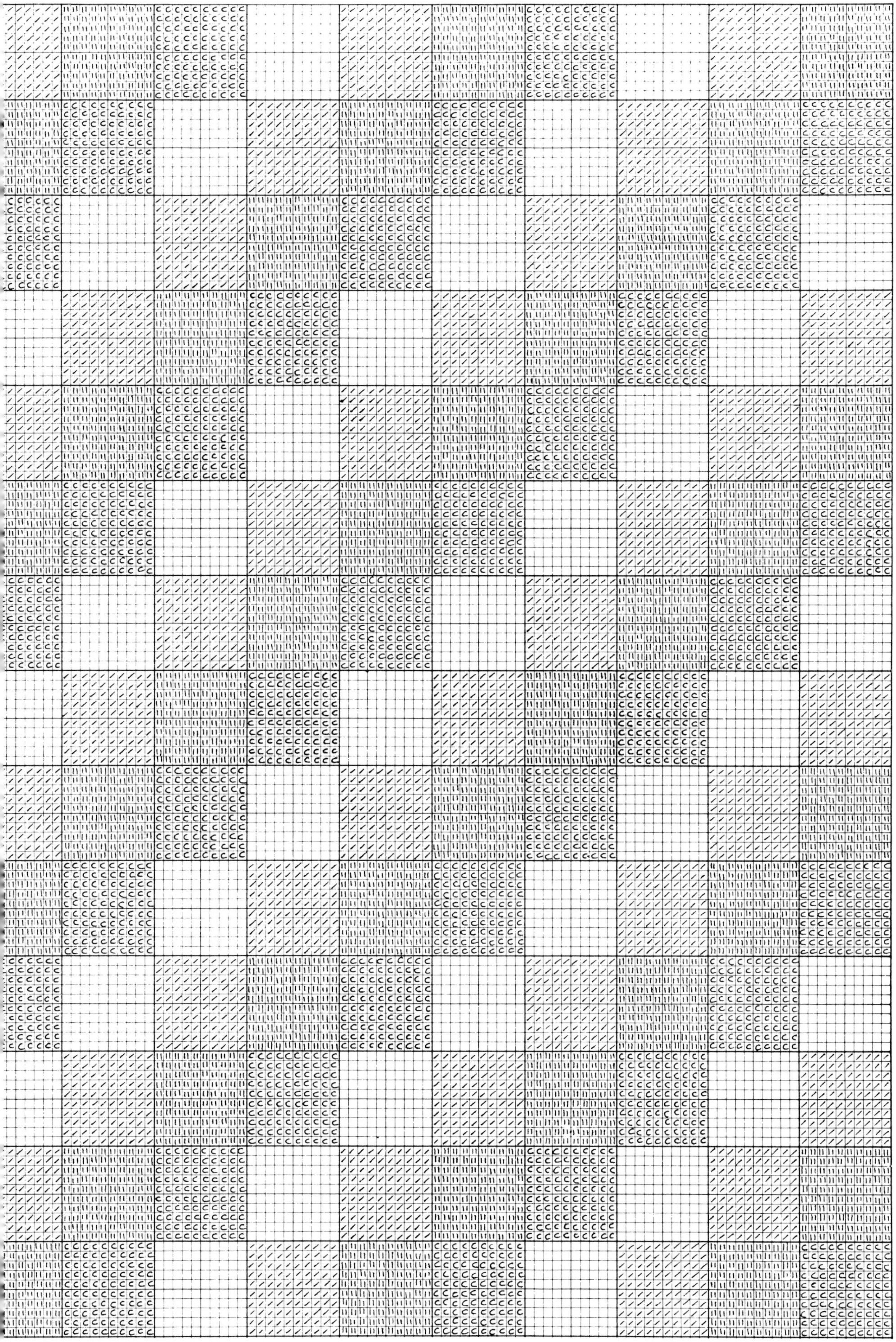

11

Leopard skin border

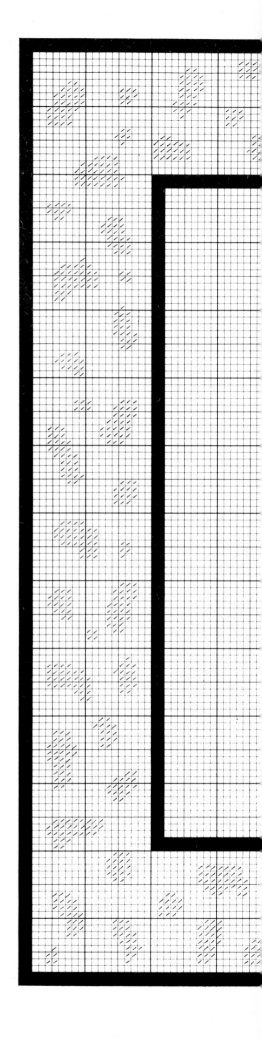

■ 7922 tan

□ 7504 yellow

☑ black

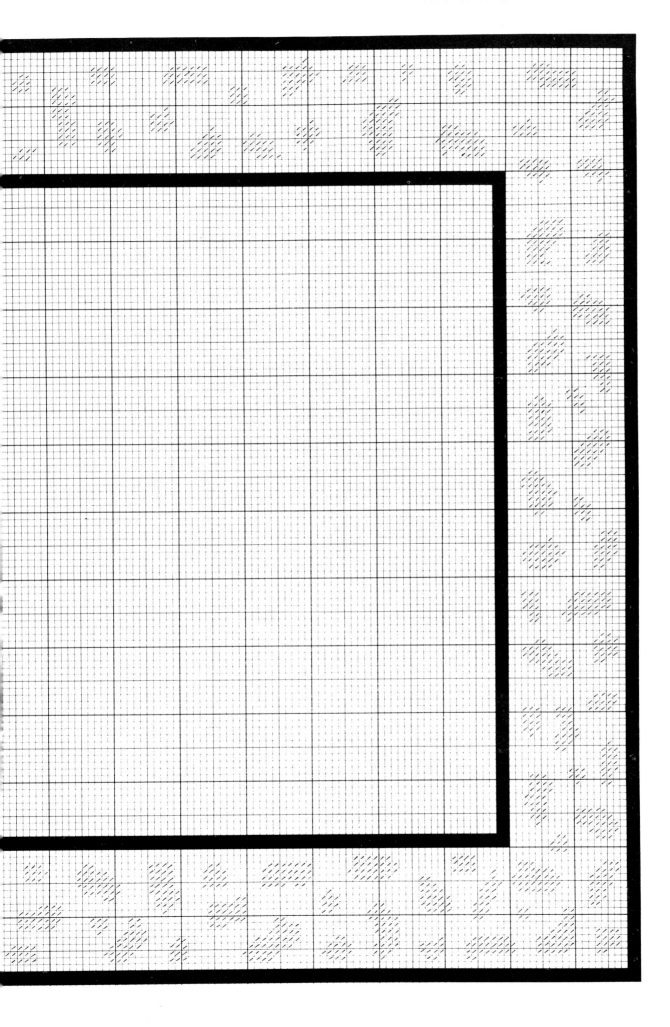

12

Modern pattern border

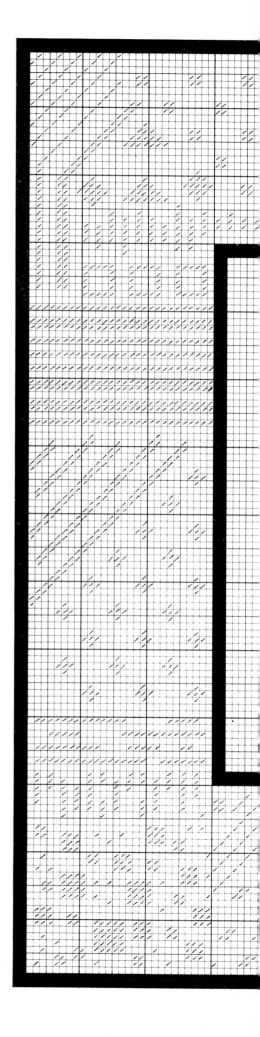

■ black

□ 7715 pale grey

 7622 dark grey

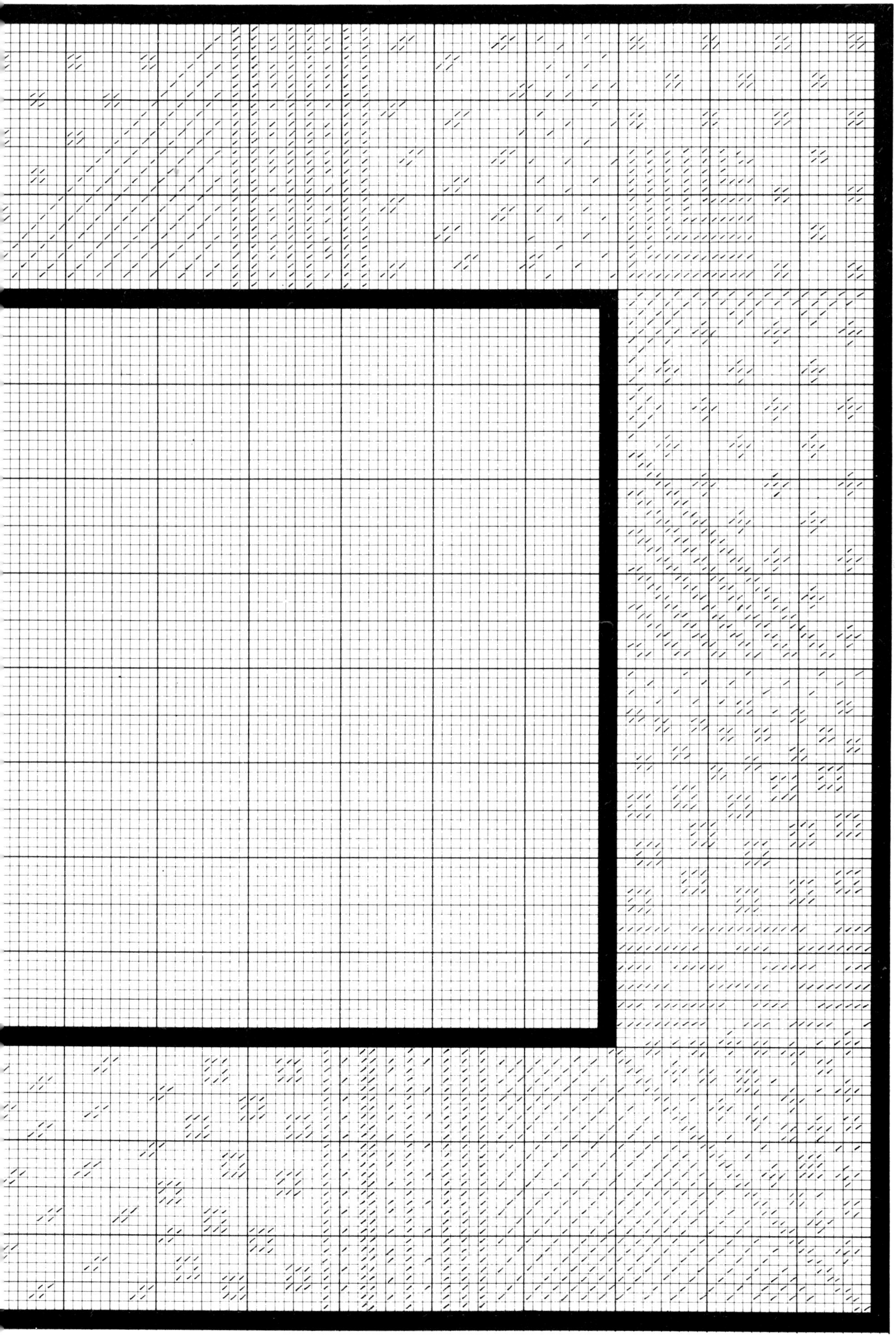

13

Tongotabu
savage tribes

☐ 7505 tan

■ black

☑ 7920 brick red

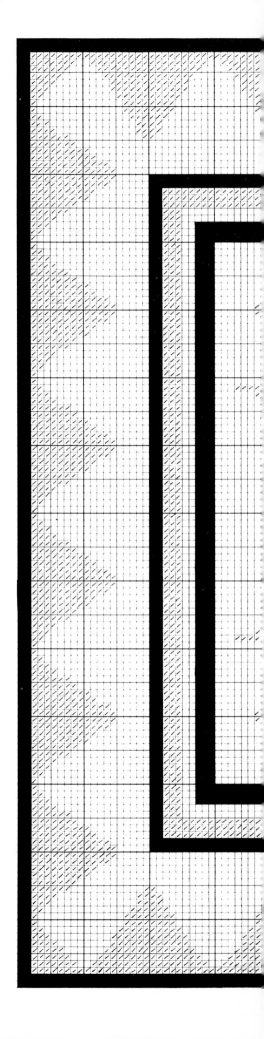

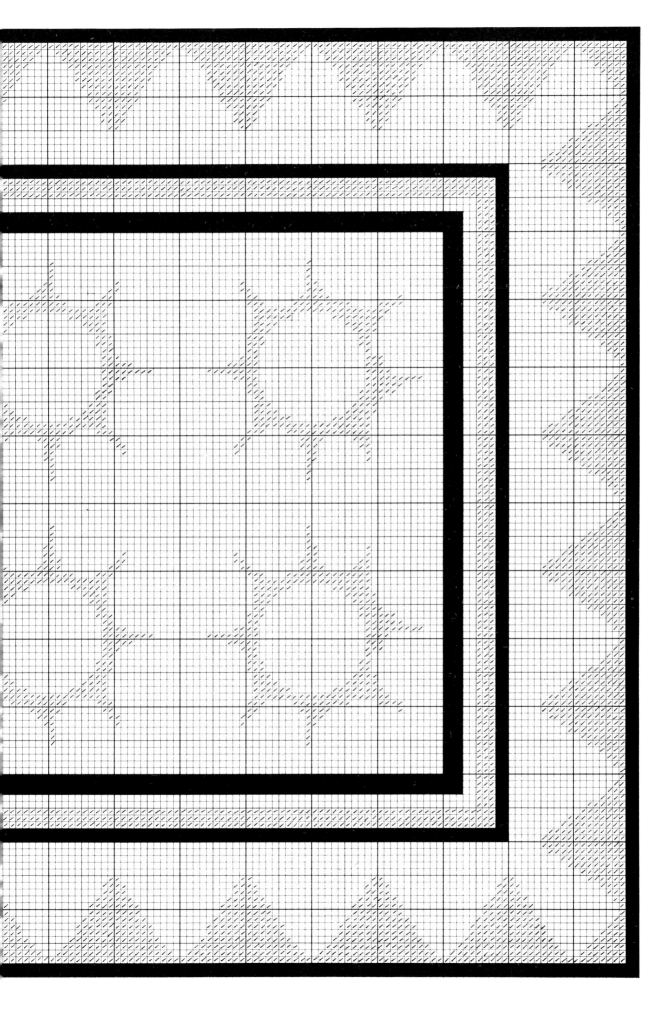

43

Swan

	black		7387 dark green
	white		7715 pale grey
	7344 green		7285 medium grey
	7740 orange		7596 medium blue/green

Photo on p.50

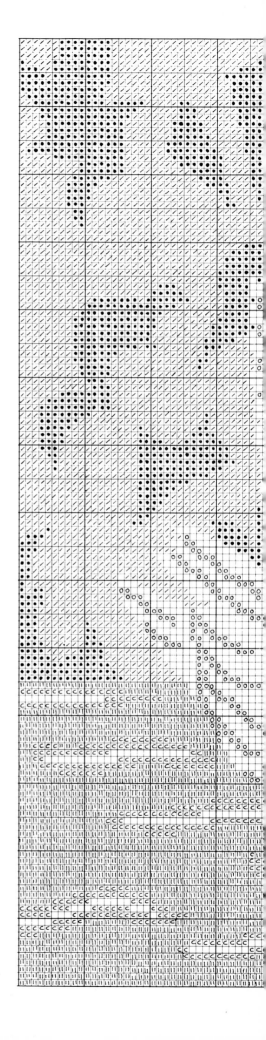

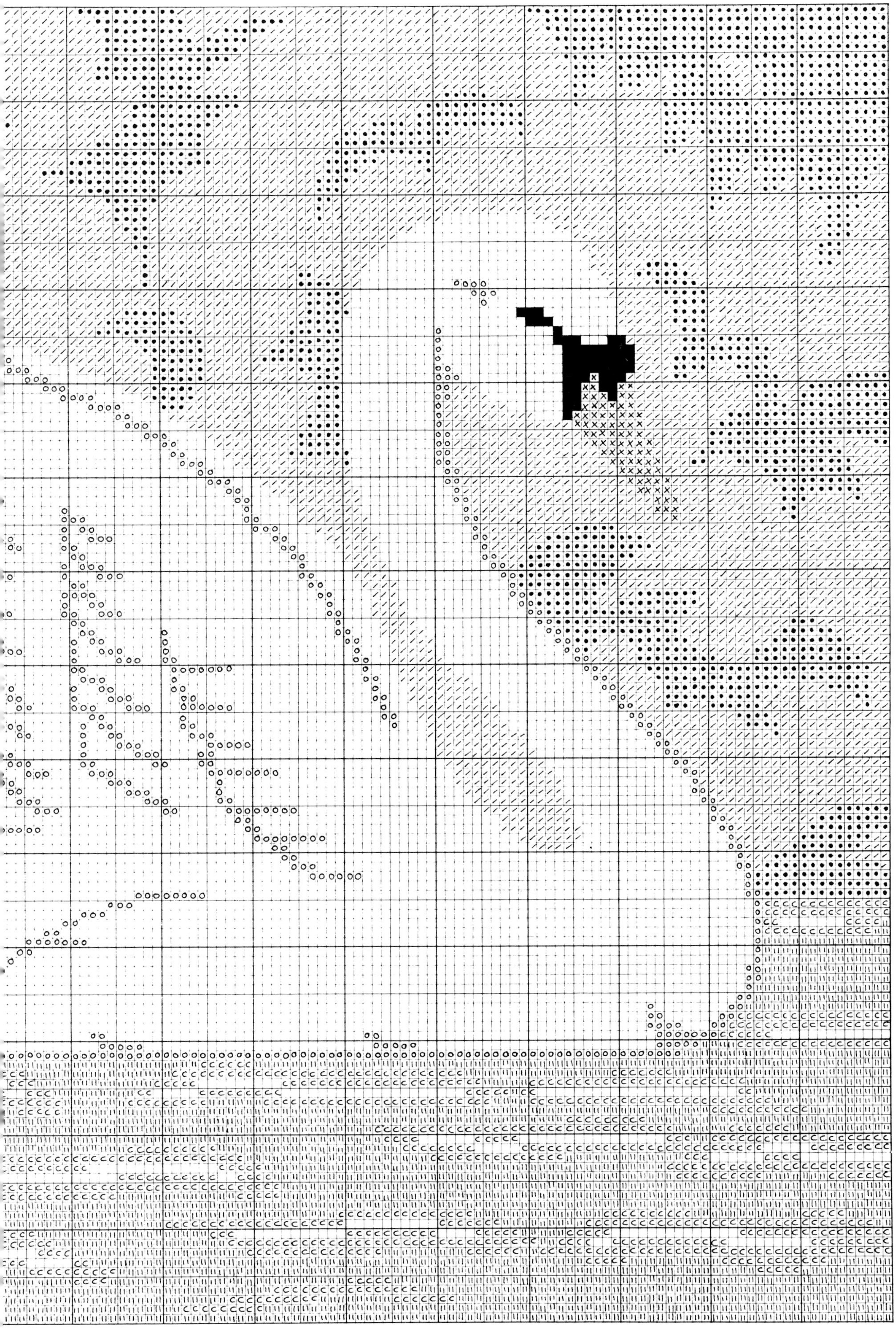

15

Roman lady

■	7245 mauve	◩ 7302	sky blue
‖	7347 dark green	◹ 7453	beige
•	7846 tan	⊠ 7911	green
□	7121 pale flesh pink	◺ 7971	dark yellow
⋁	7852 pink	C 7437	orange

Photo on p.51

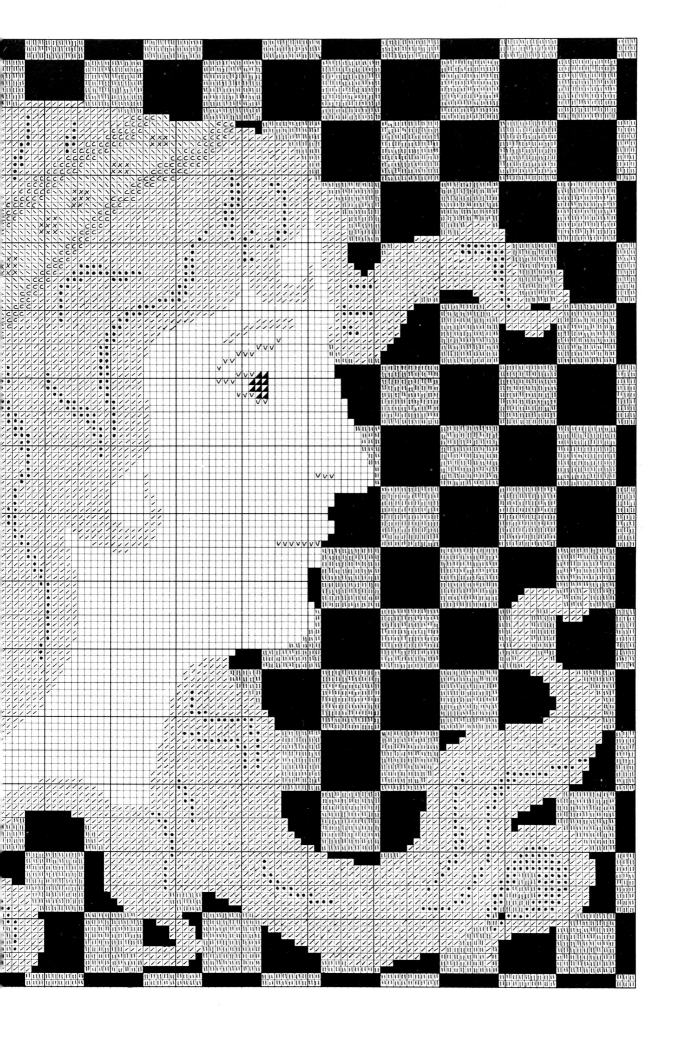

16

Doves of love

black

7951 dusky pink

C 7715 pale grey

× 7376 pistachio green

• 7518 light brown

7424 light pistachio green

· white

Photo on p.51

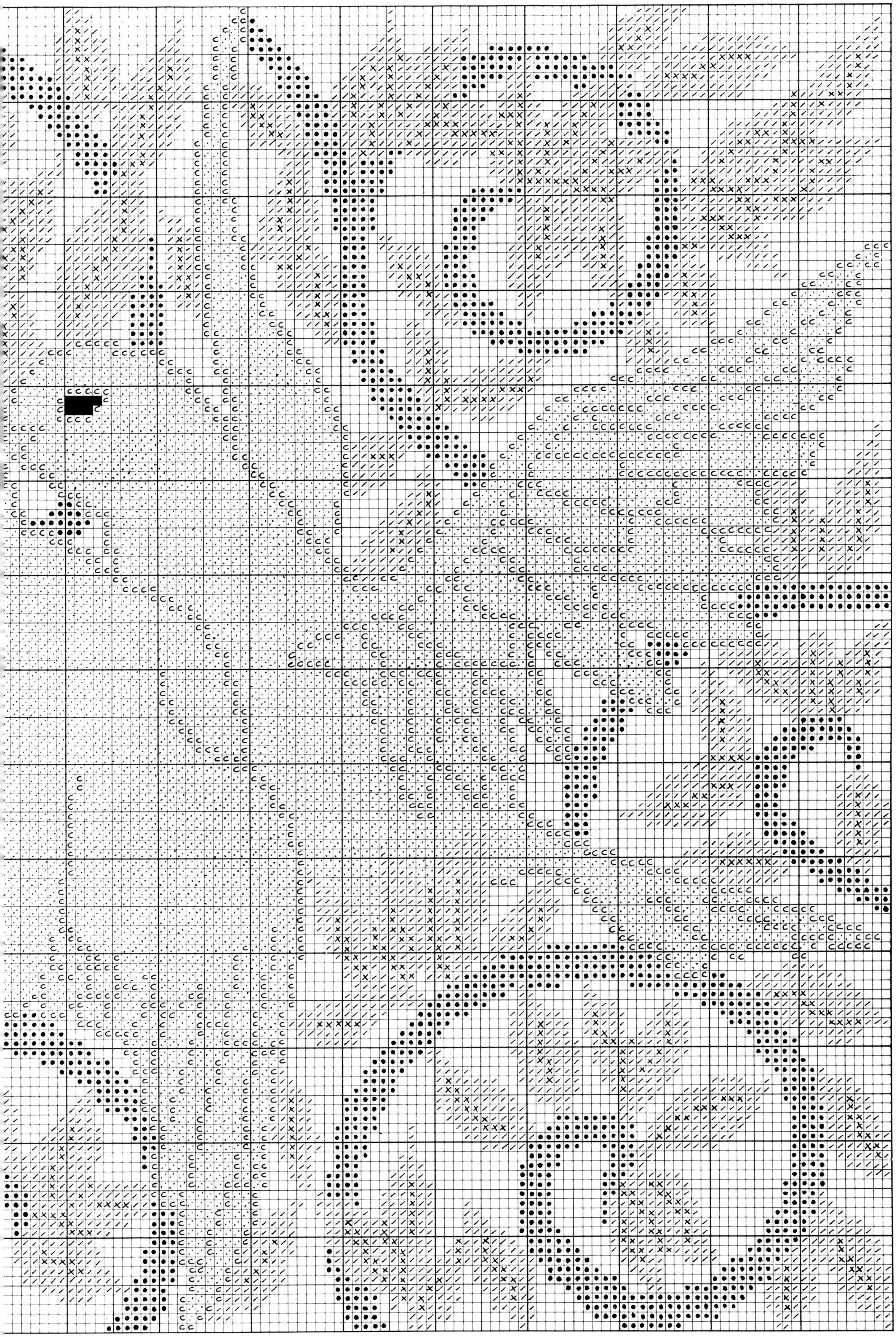

Swan

See p.44

Roman Lady

See p.46

Doves of love

See p.48

Cottage in the country

	black		7823	royal blue
	7799	sky blue		7666	red
	7184	brick red		7435	yellow
	white		7176	light rust
	7341	bright green		7345	medium green
	7469	dark brown		7622	dark grey
	7462	beige		7715	pale grey
	7804	rose pink		7491	cream
	7348	dark green			

Photo on p.54

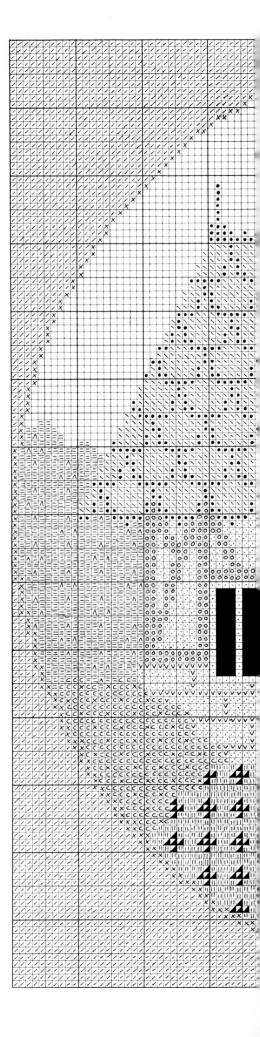

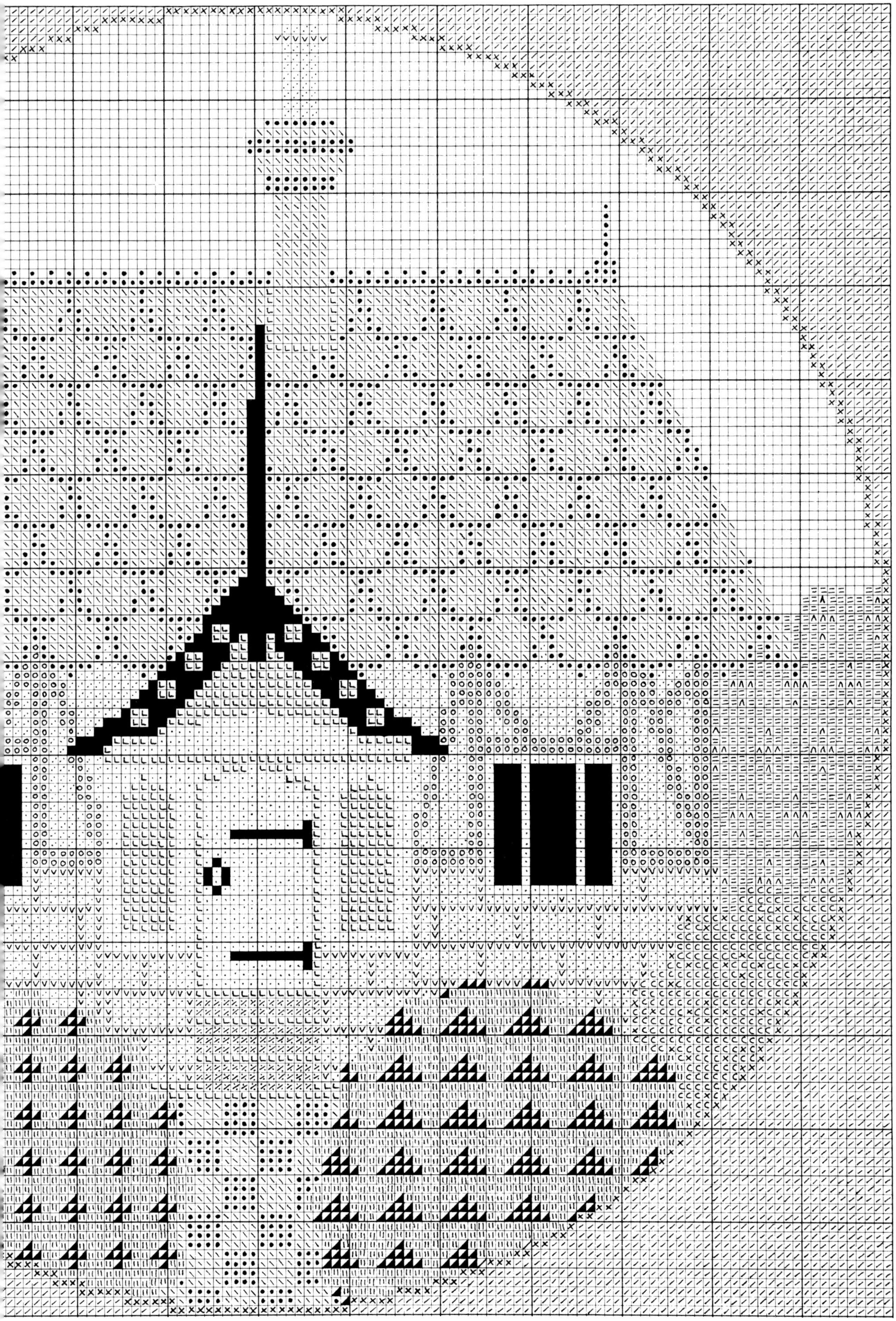

Greek pattern (1)
See p.56

Cottage in the country
See p.52

18

Greek pattern (1)

	black	☐	7437 orange
●	7401 brown	‖	7504 yellow

Photo on p.55

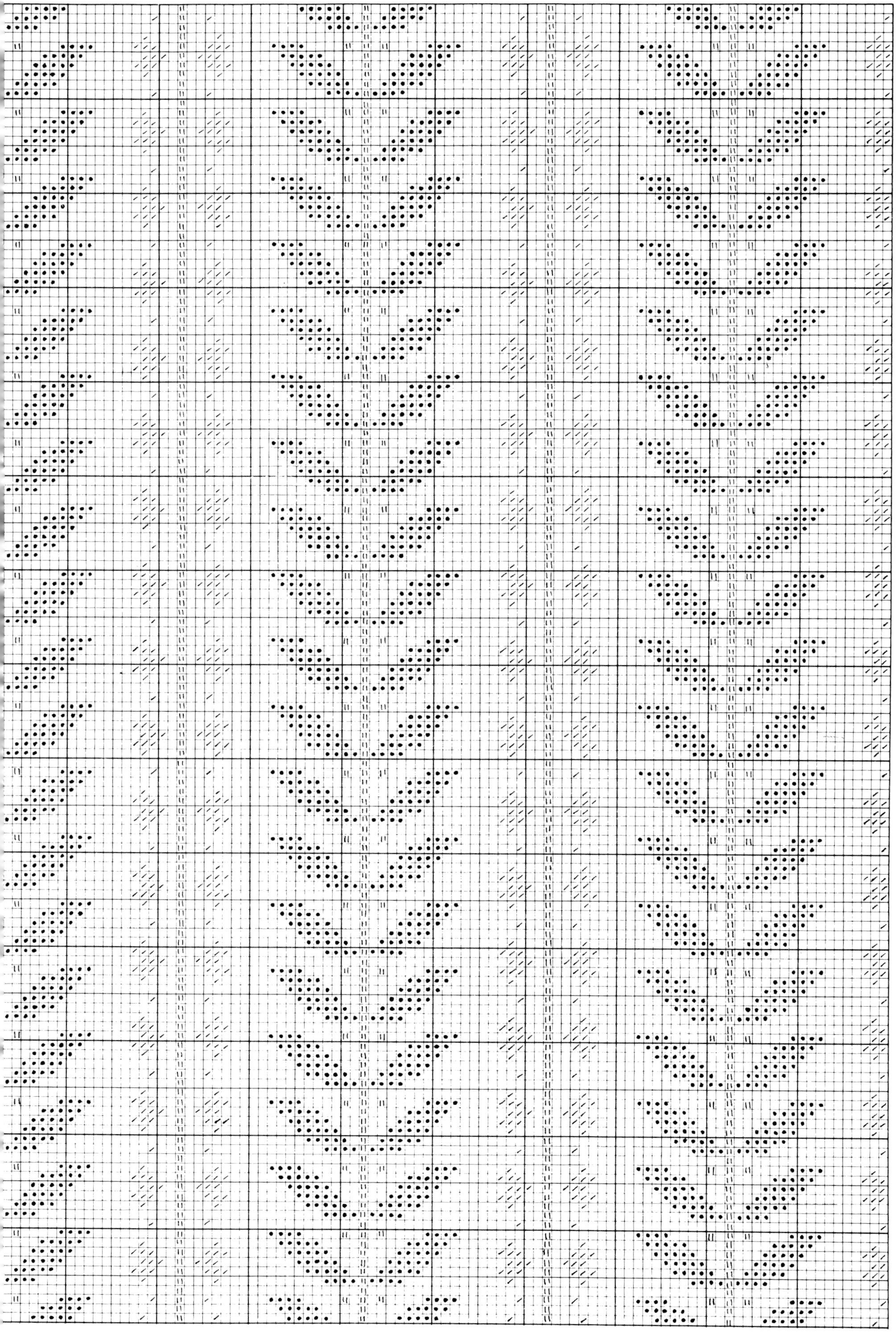

19

Greek pattern (2)

☐ black

☑ 7504 yellow

⊞ 7920 brick red

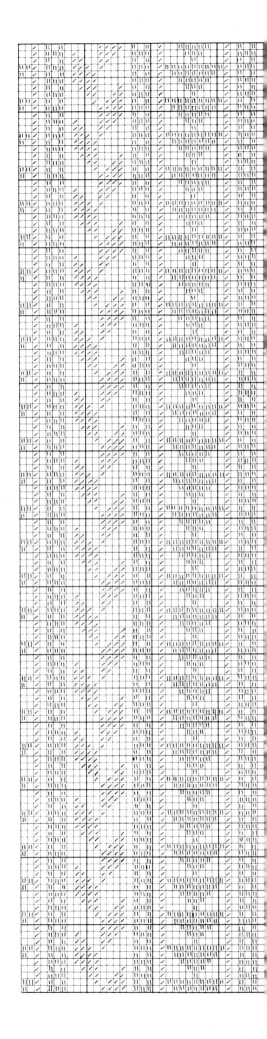

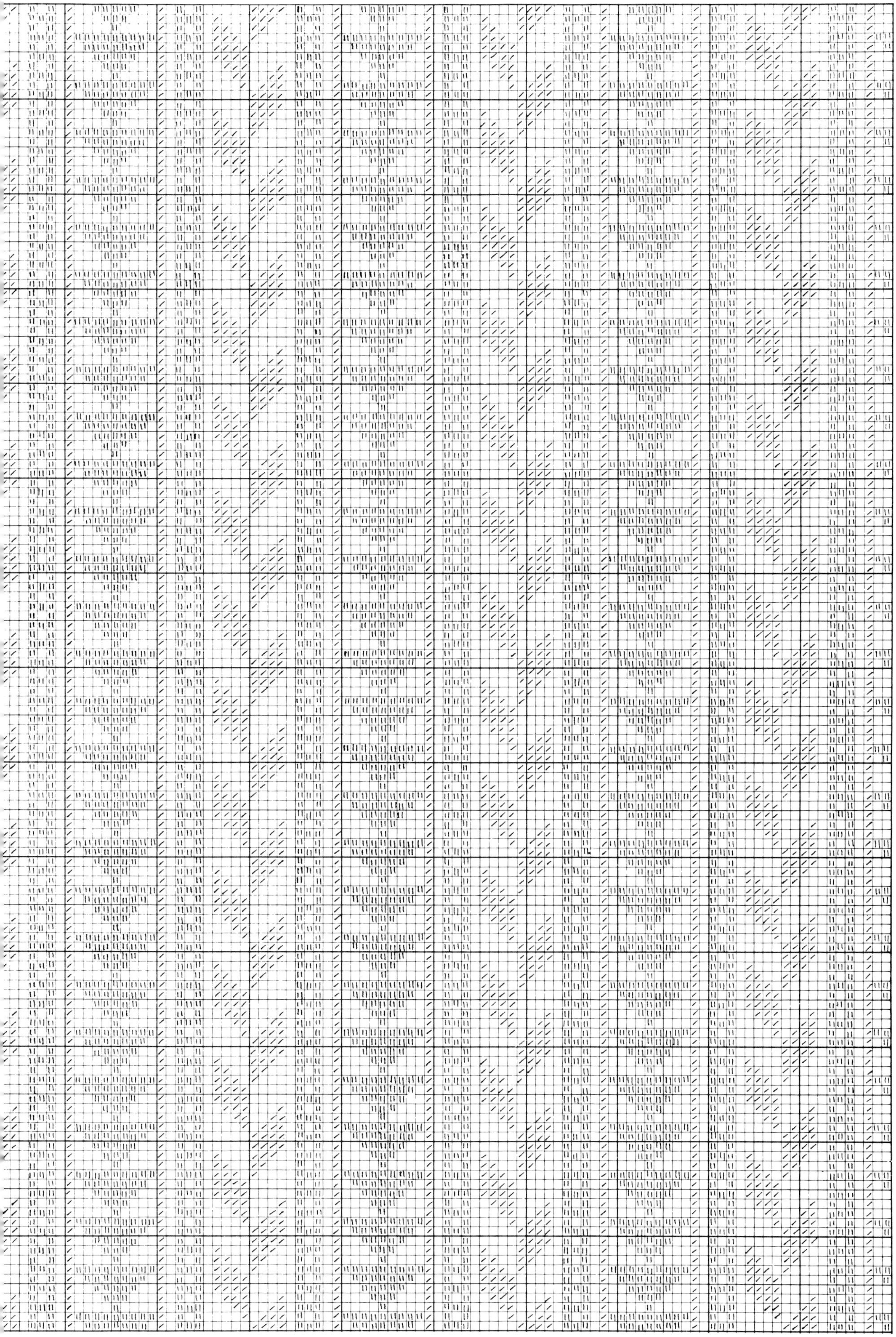

20

Modern geometric pattern (1)

☑ black   C̲ 7666 red

☐ white   ⫶ 7715 pale grey

⊞ 7622 dark grey

Photo on p.62

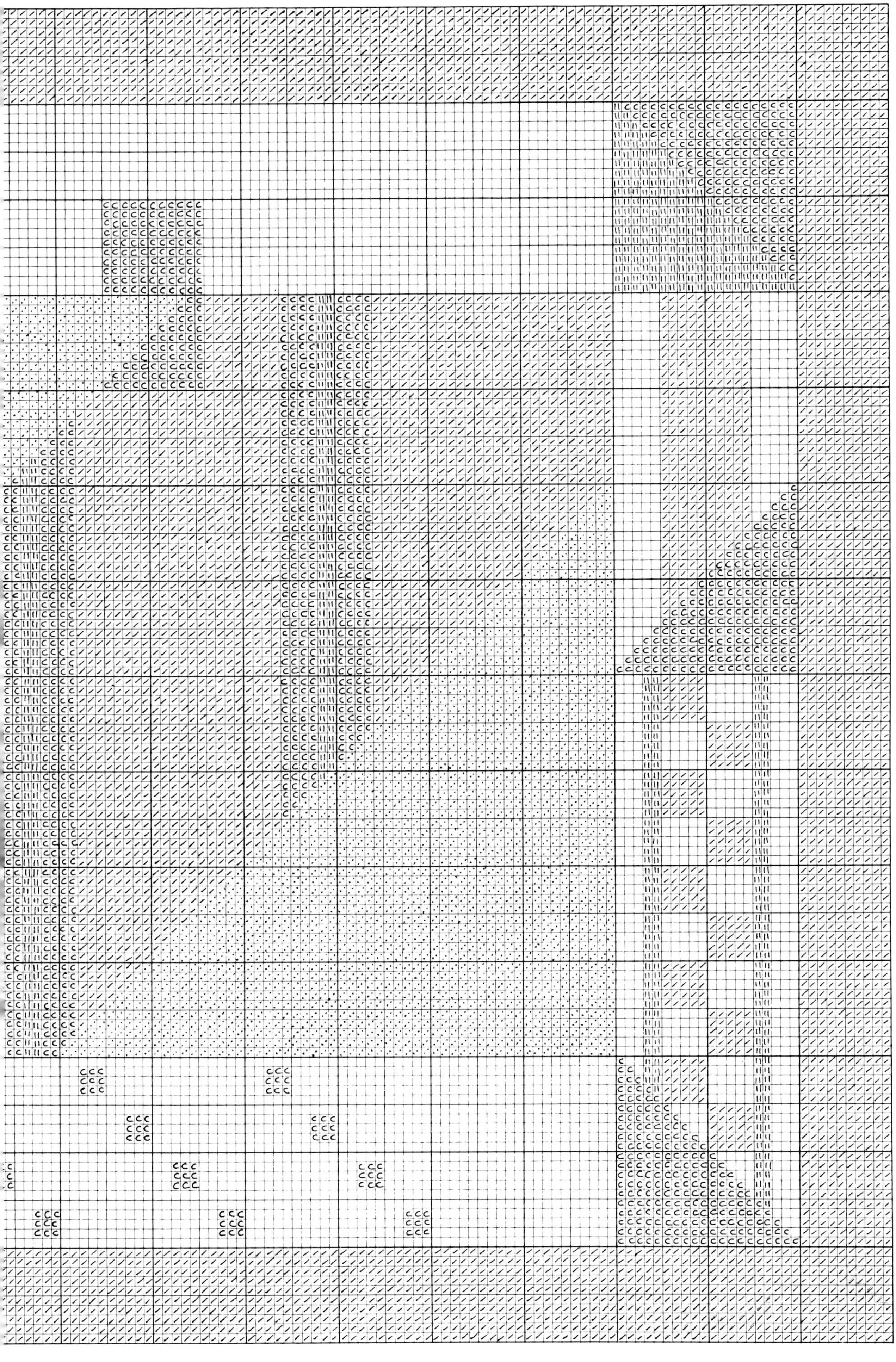

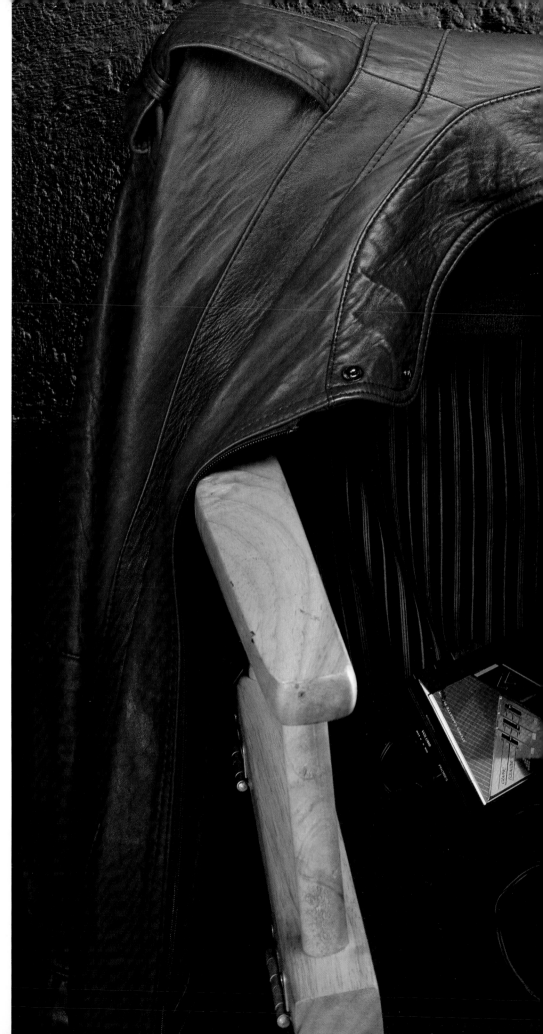

Modern
geometric pattern (1)
See p.60

21

Modern geometric pattern (2)

	white		7715 pale grey
■	7622 dark grey	•	black
⊘	7666 red		

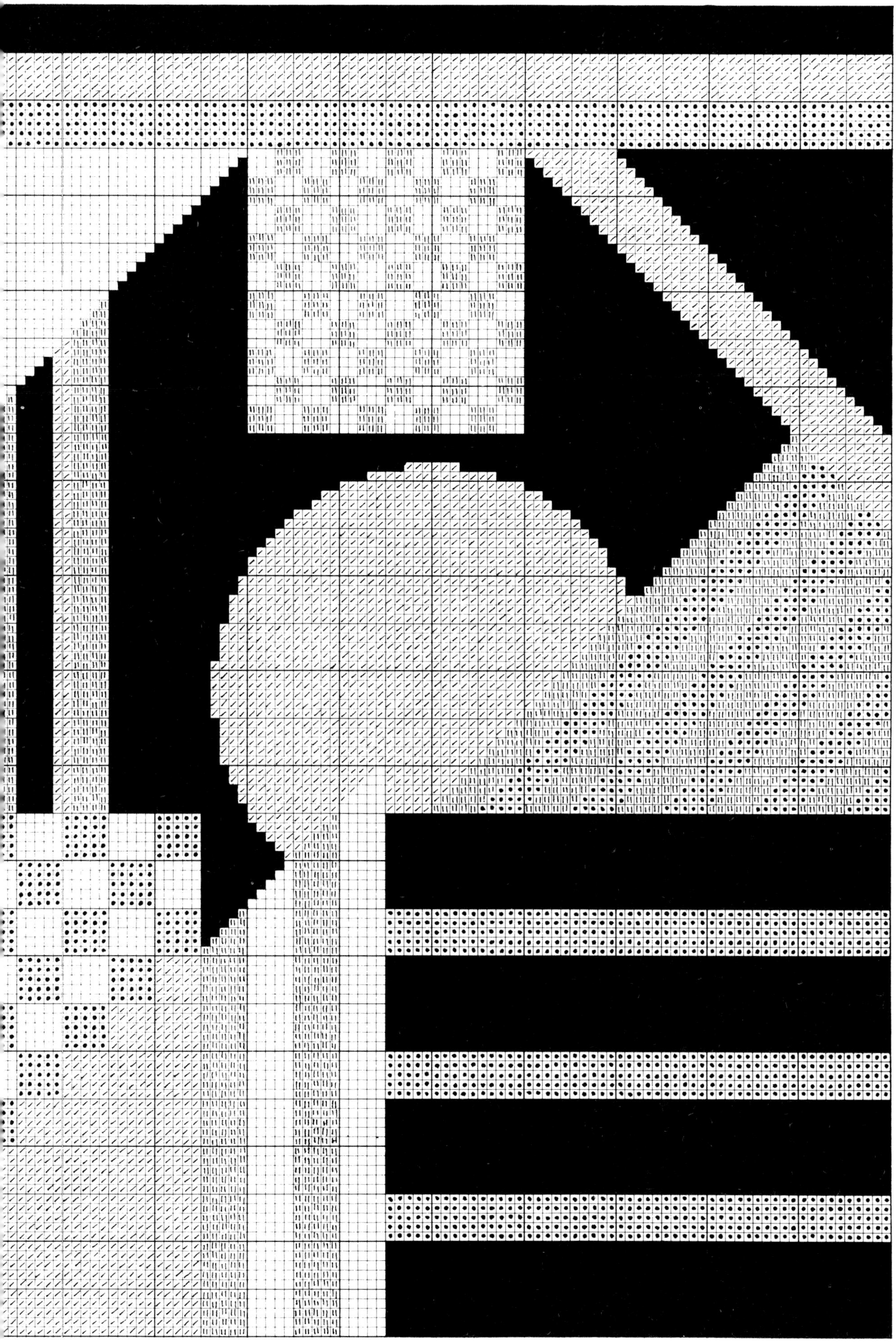

22

Windmill pattern

 7709 lilac

■ 7713 dark pewter grey

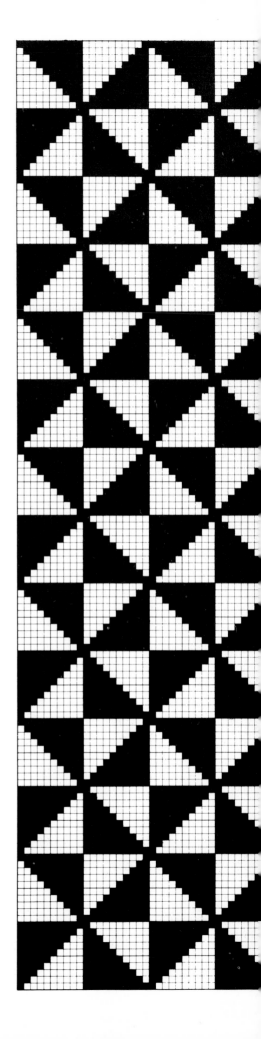

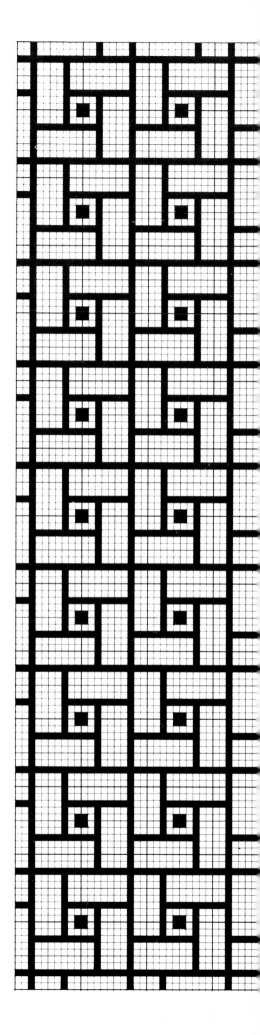

23

Pompeiian pattern

 7920 brick red

■ black

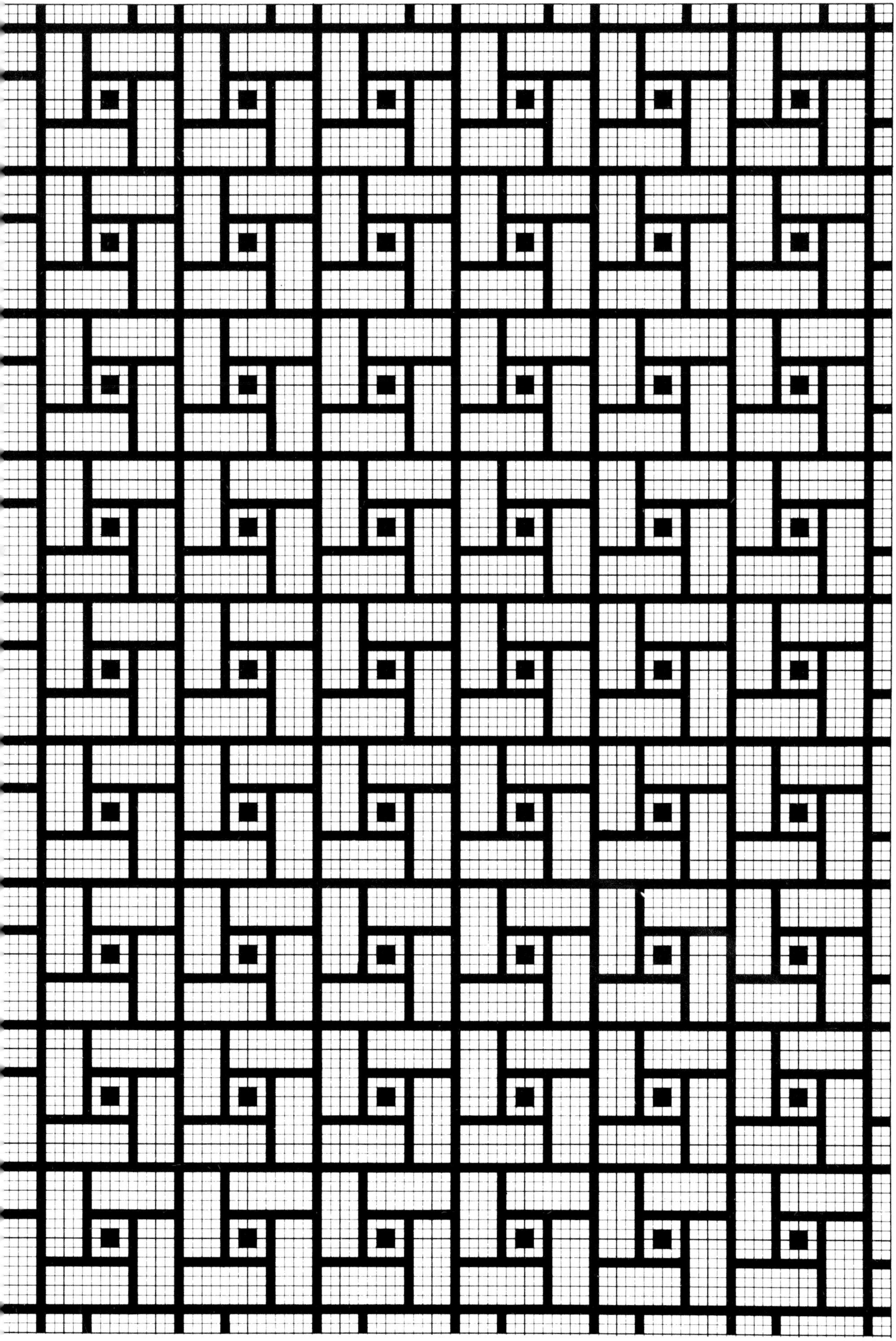

24

Patchwork

■ 7895 lilac

☐ 7820 royal blue

⊡ 7852 pink

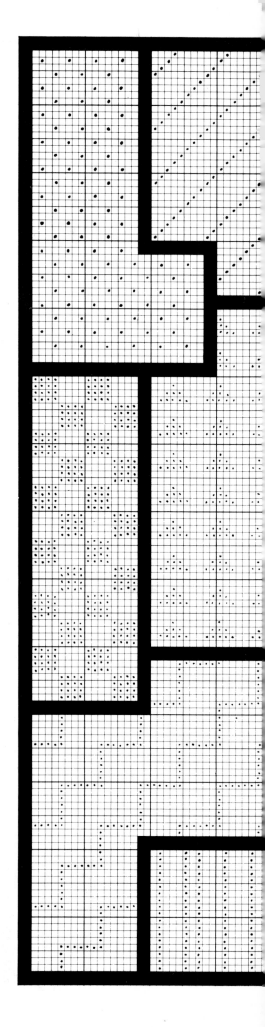

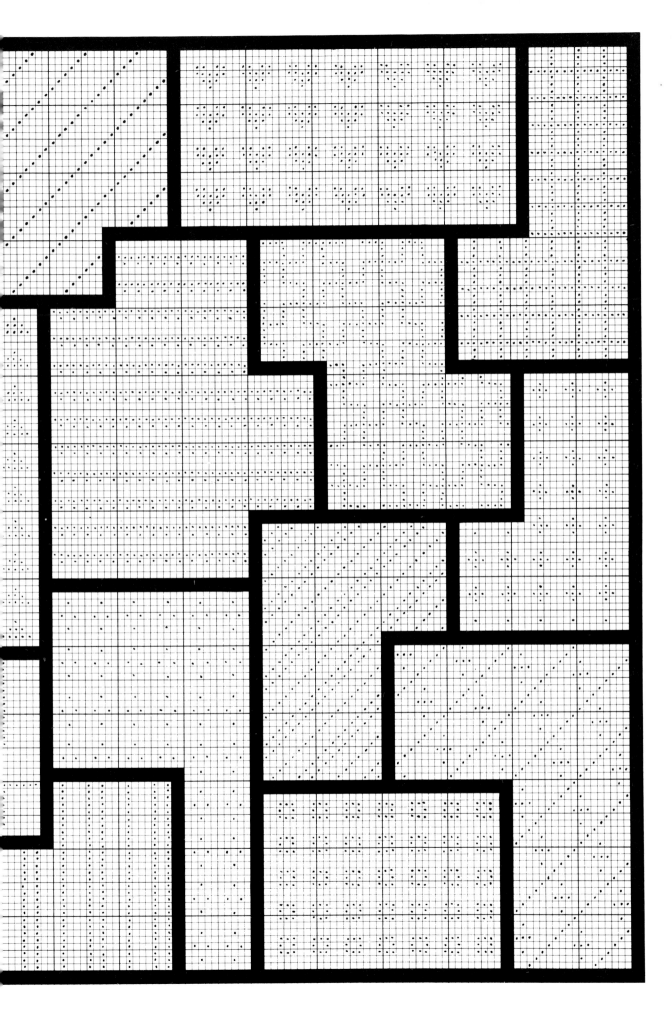

Hearts

☐ black
 7666 red

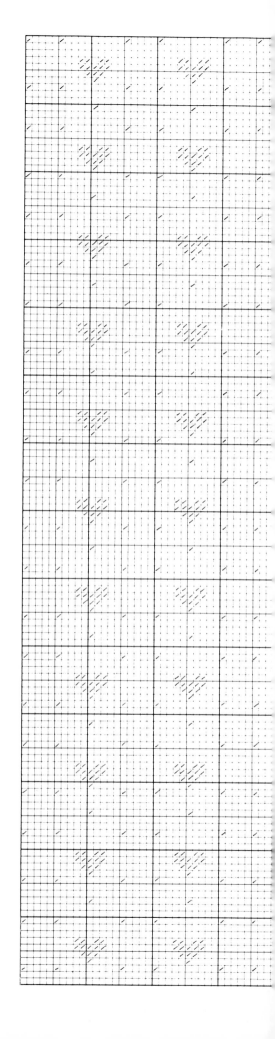

26

Rose garden (1)

■ 7911	green	⧄ 7605	rose pink
□	black	⊡ 7600	dark rose pink

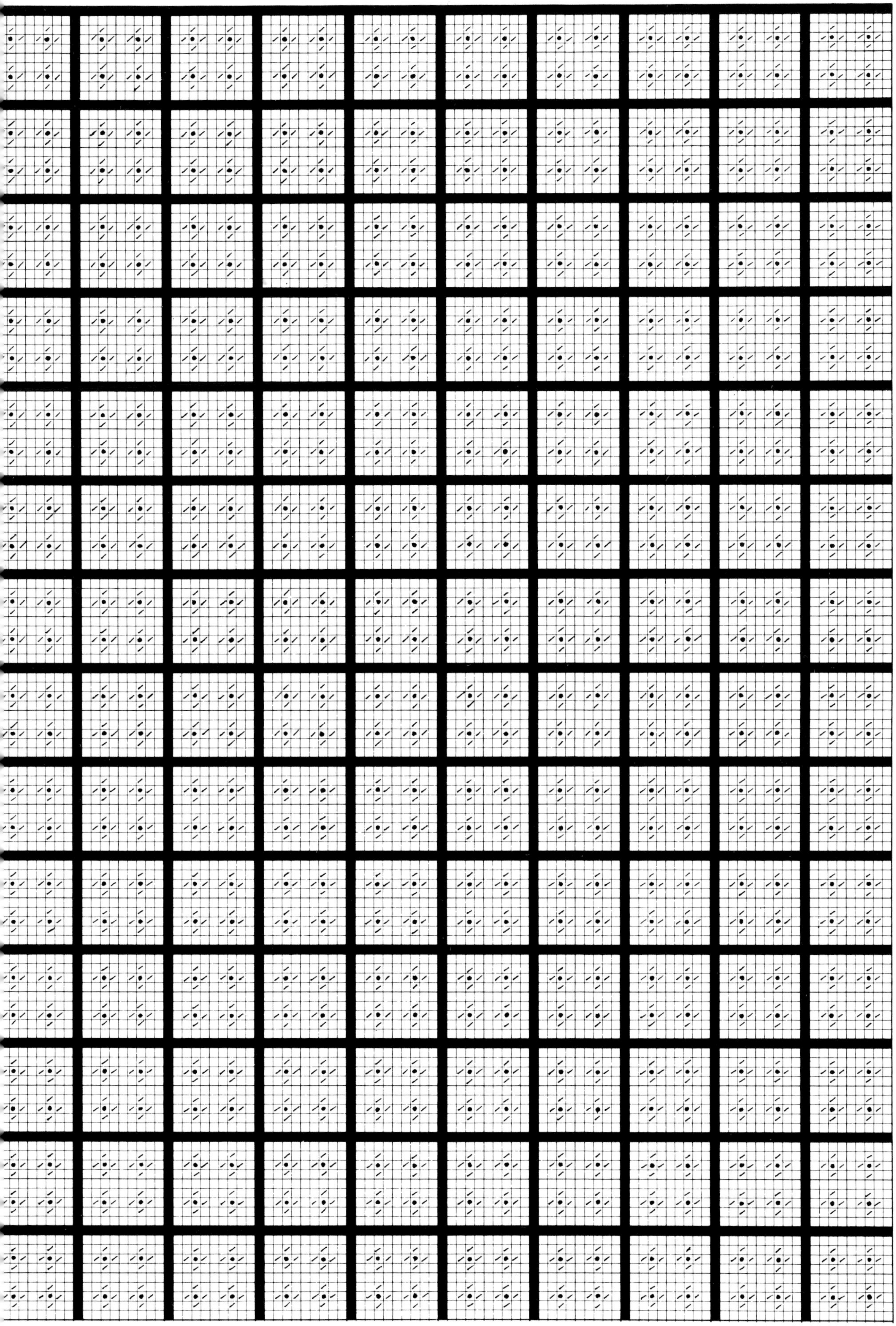

Rose garden (2)

• 7600 dark rose pink		☑ 7605 rose pink
☐ black		☒ 7911 green

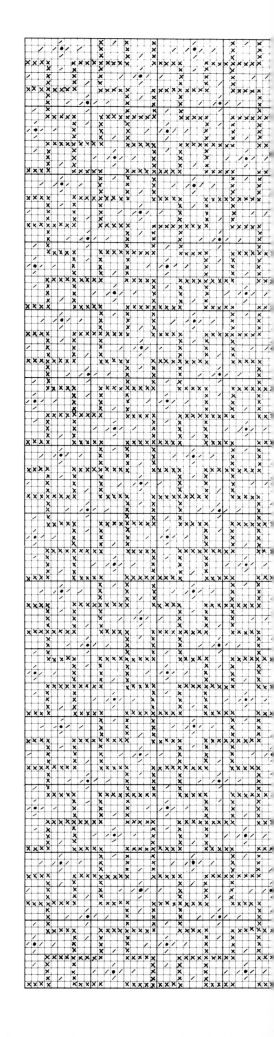

28

Egyptian pattern (1)

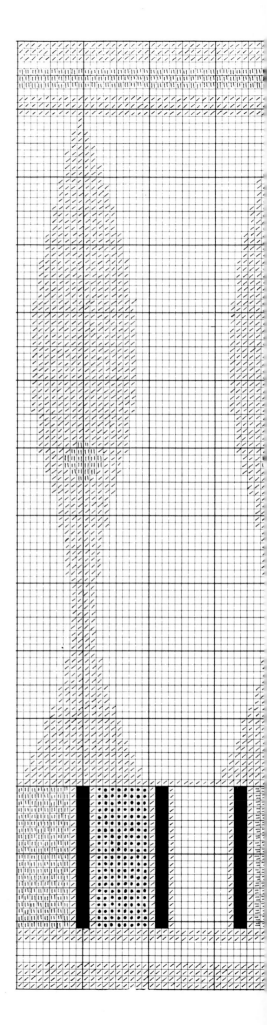

☐ 7742 dark yellow	‖ 7666 red
■ white	• 7620 medium grey
╱ black	═ 7547 green

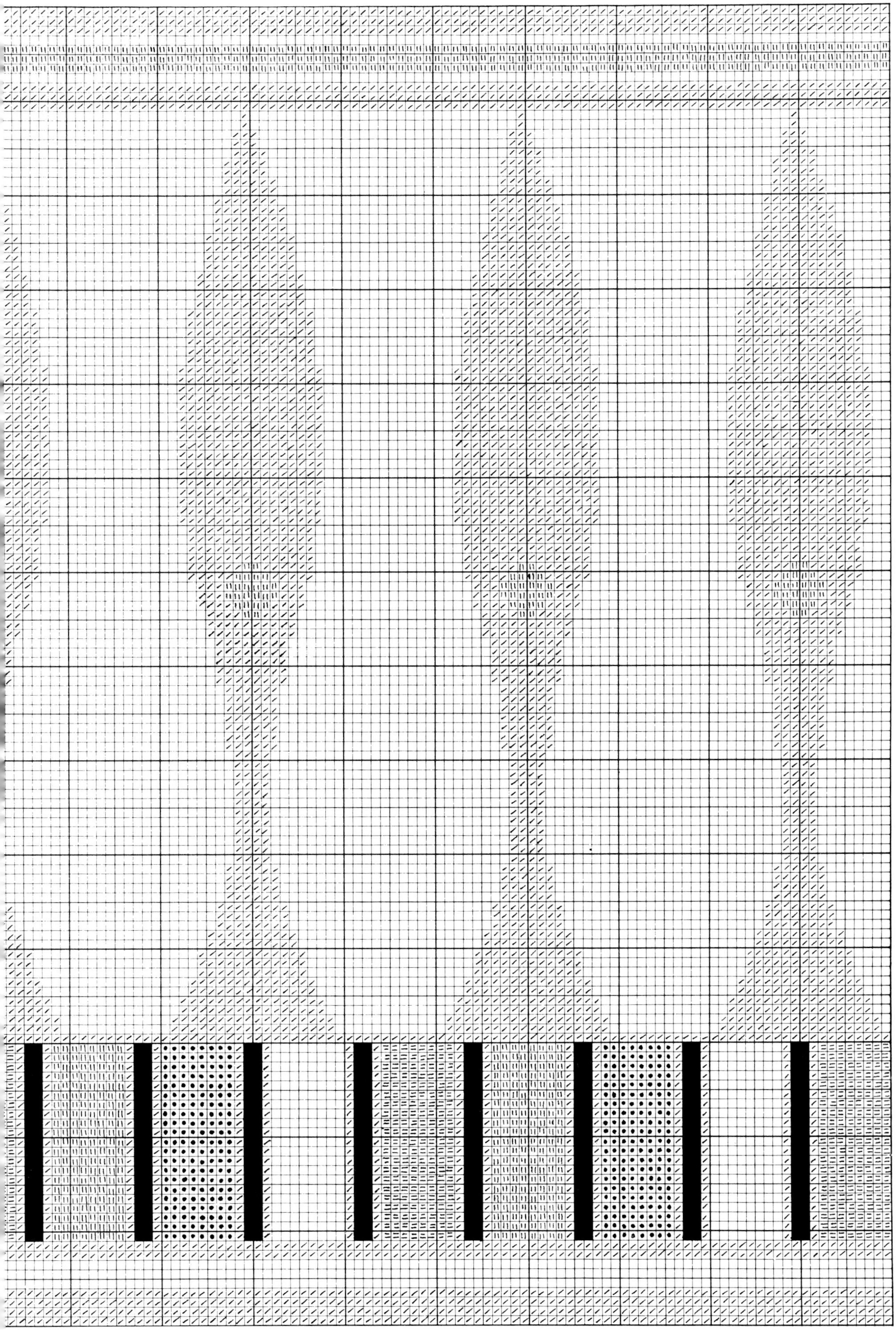

29

Egyptian pattern (2)

☐ 7742 dark yellow ‖ 7245 mauve

• 7920 brick red C black

╱ 7547 green

Photo on p.82

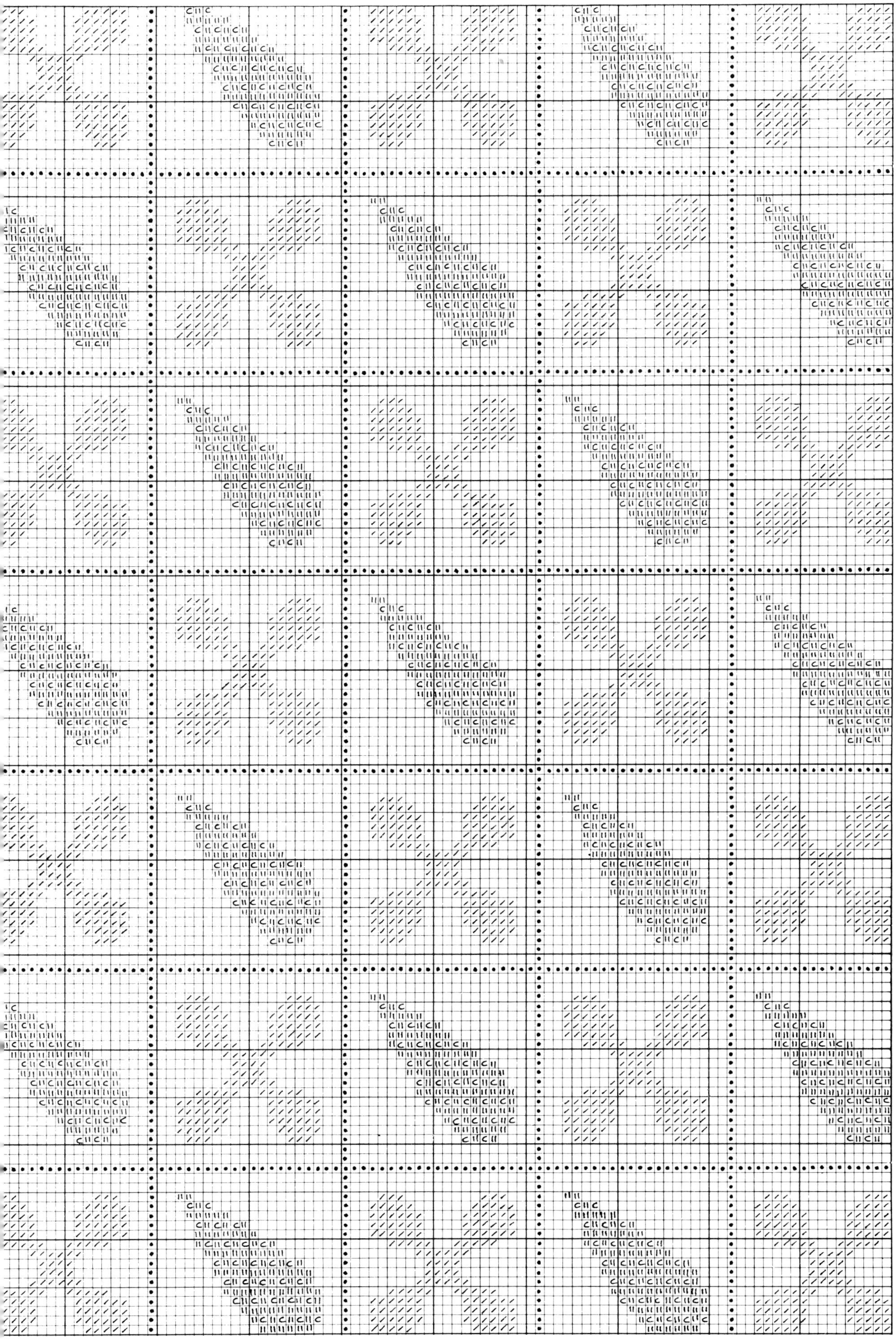

Egyptian pattern (3)

See p.84

Egyptian pattern (2)

See p.80

30

Egyptian pattern (3)

		7666 red			7742 dark yellow
		7346 green			white
		7503 creamy yellow			

Photo on p.83

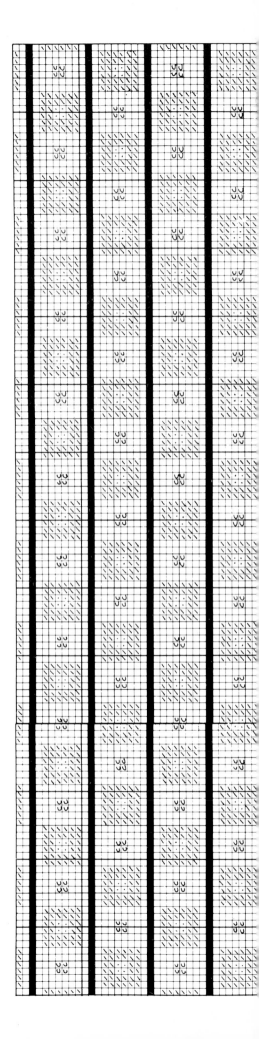

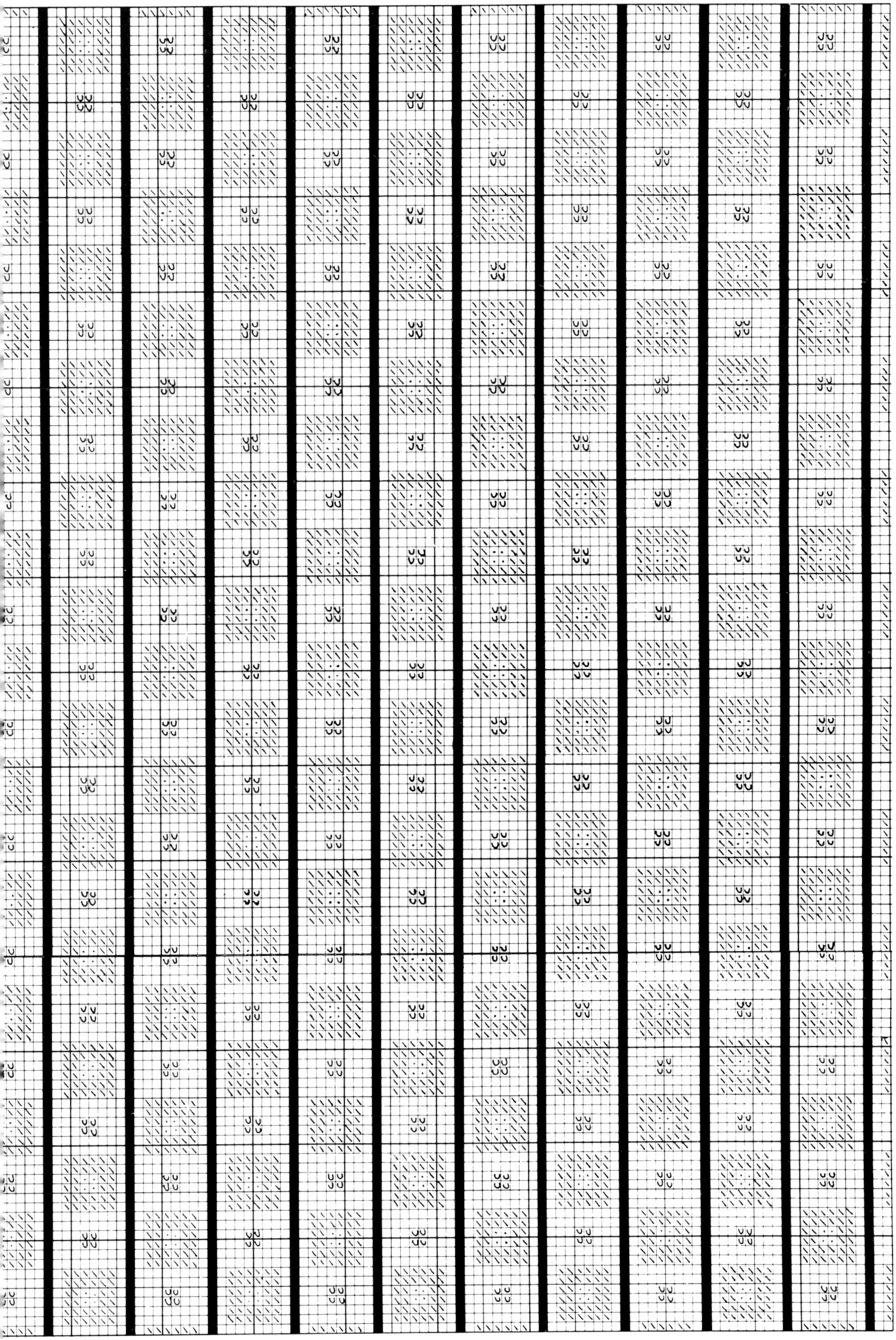

31

Egyptian pattern (4)

☐ 7547 green

☑ 7742 dark yellow

Ⅲ 7920 brick red

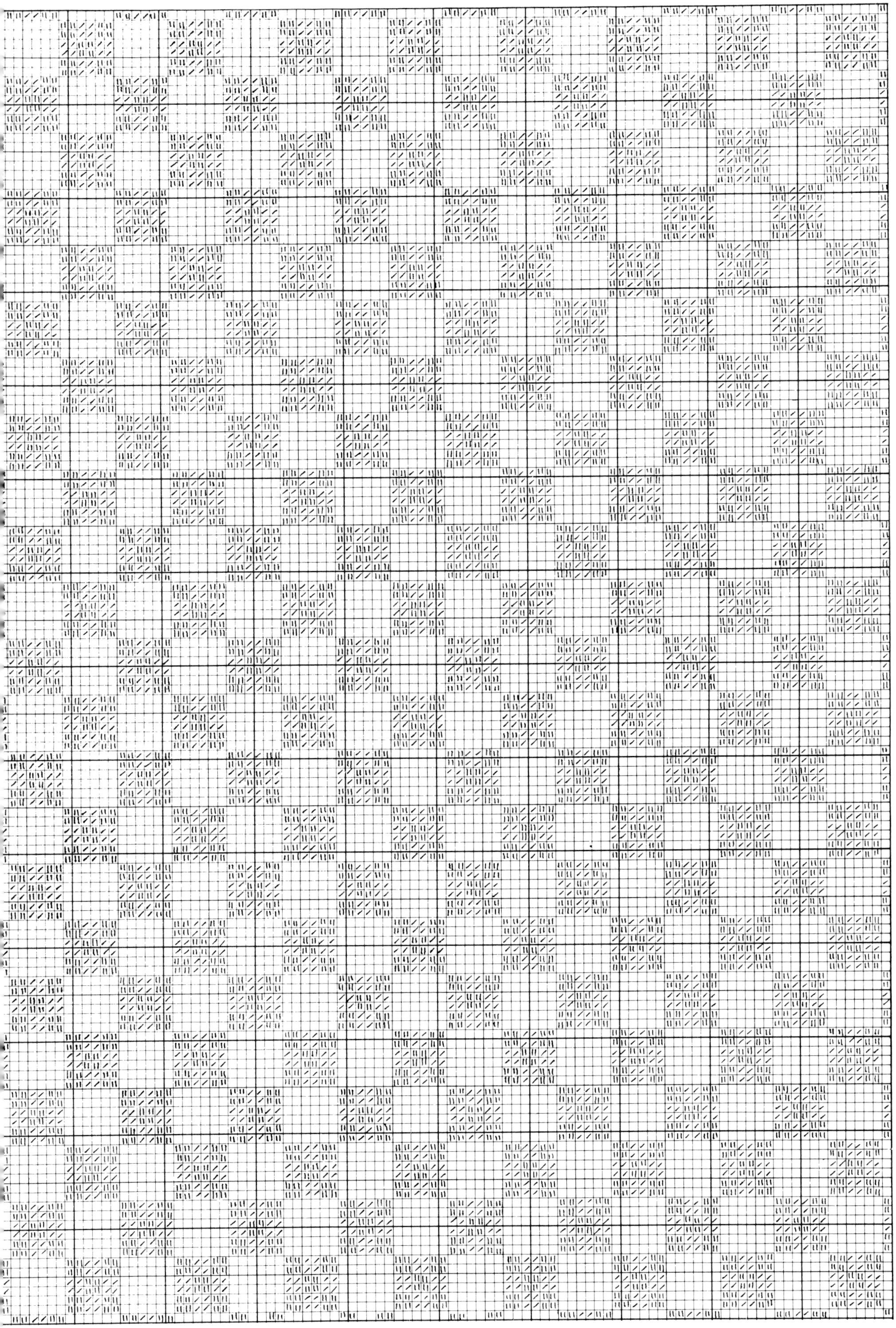

Floral border repeat

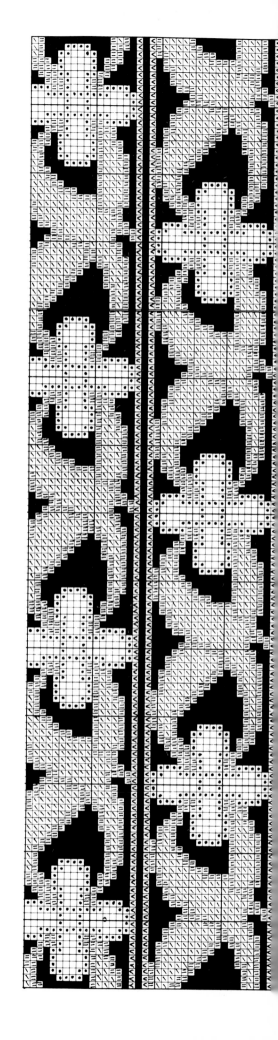

□	7314 sky blue	◢	7911 green
■	black	☰	7472 pale mustard yellow
⊡	7600 dark rose pink	◿	7474 mustard

Photo on p.90

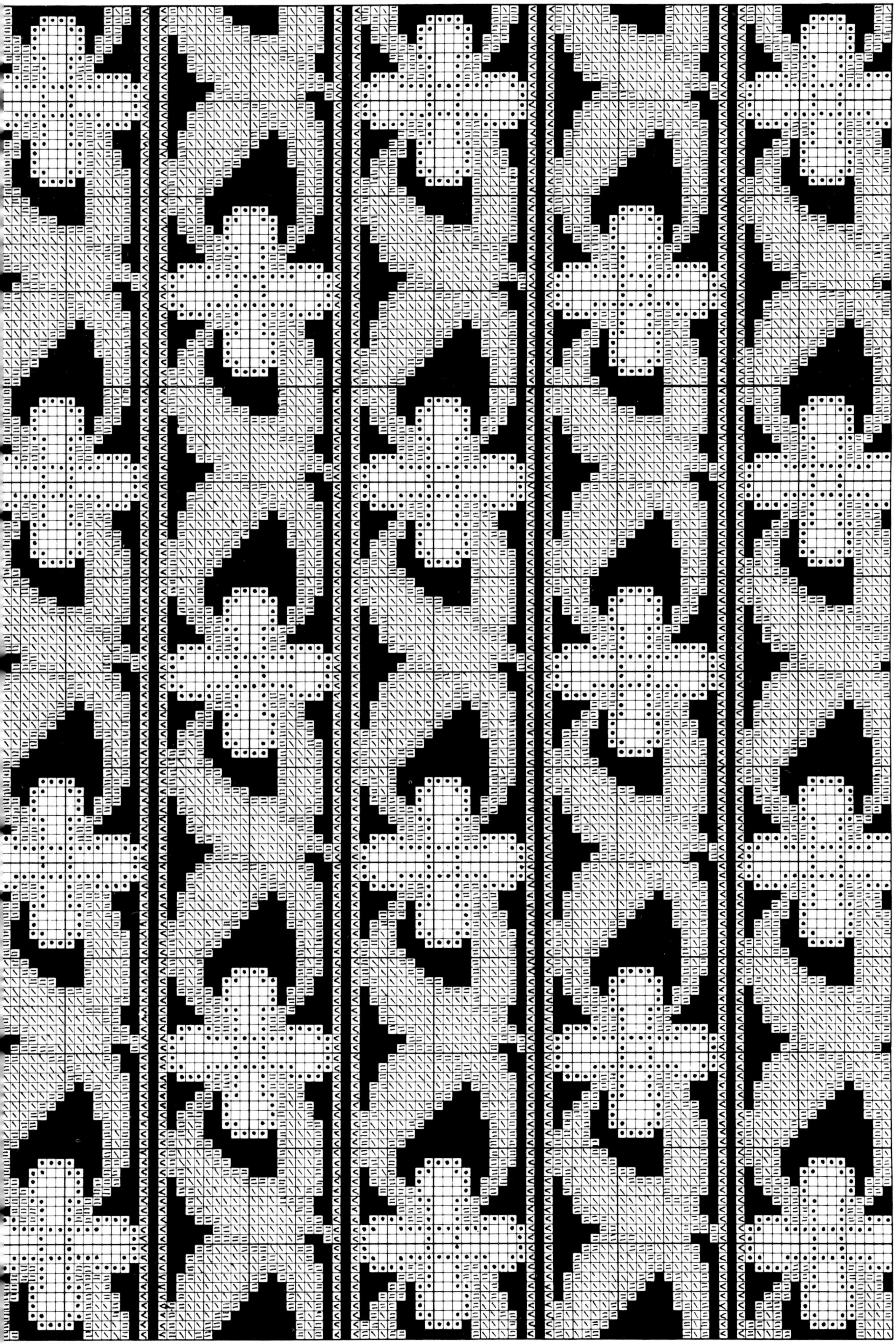

Floral border repeat

See p.88

33

Persian floral pattern (1)

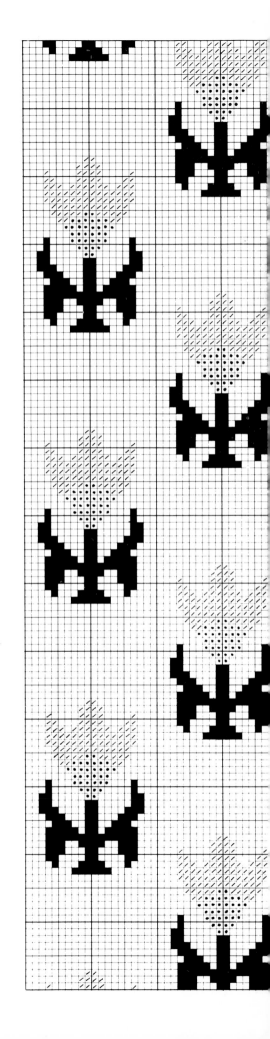

■ 7348 dark green	⊡ 7133 pink
□ 7341 bright green	▨ 7600 dark rose pink

Photo on p.94

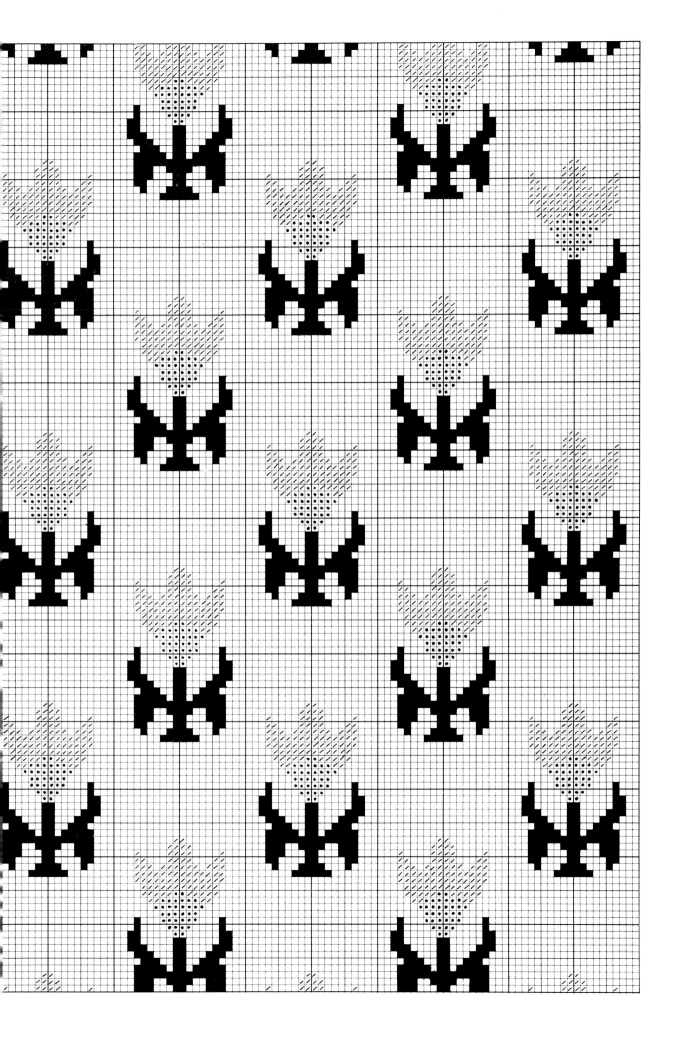

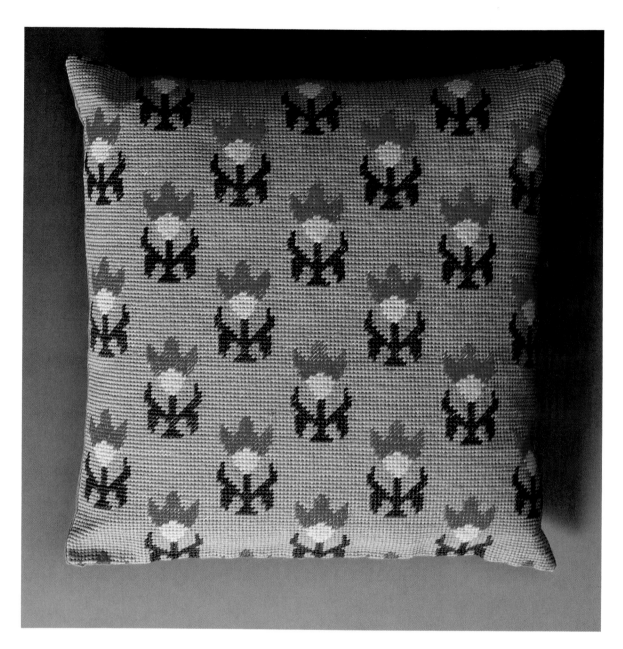

Persian floral pattern (1)
See p.92

Persian floral pattern (2)
See p.96

34

Persian floral pattern (2)

■ 7345 medium green

☐ 7786 yellow

☑ 7849 red

Photo on p.95

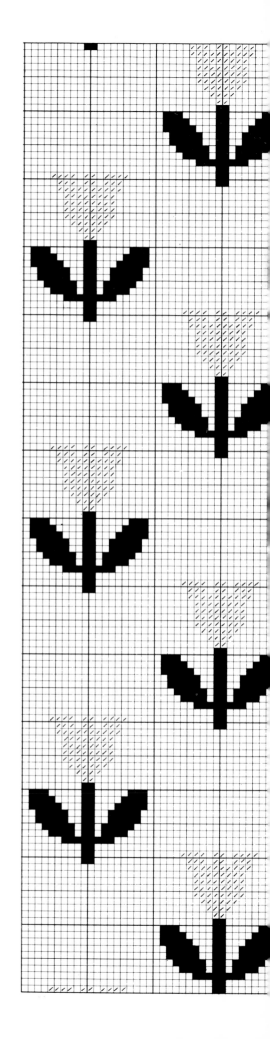

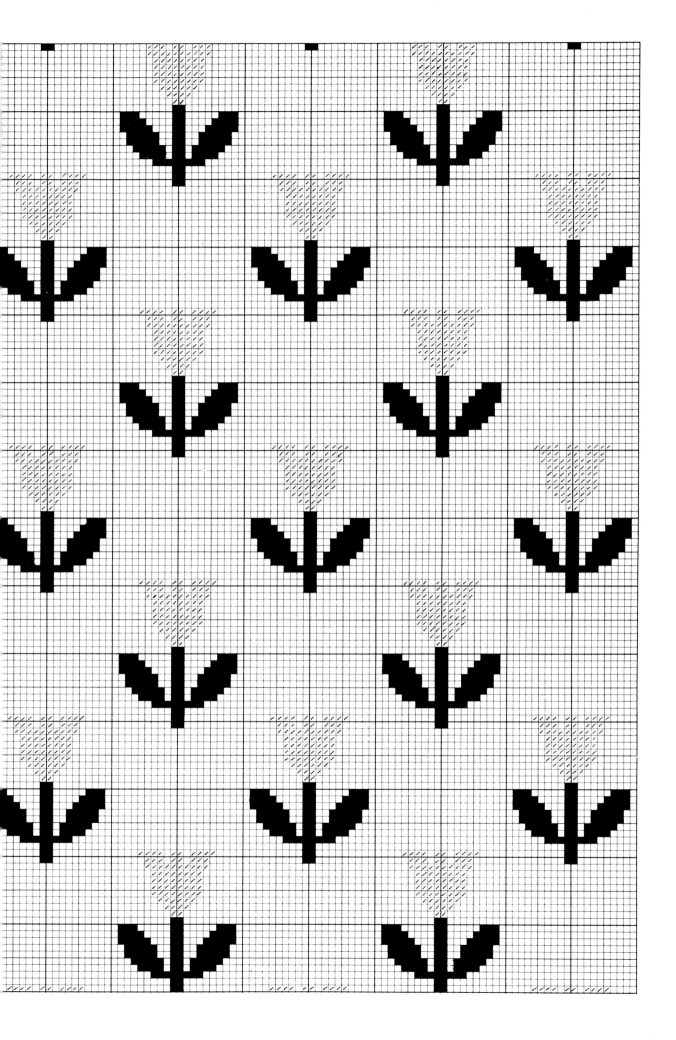

35

Flowers
and
ribbons

□ black	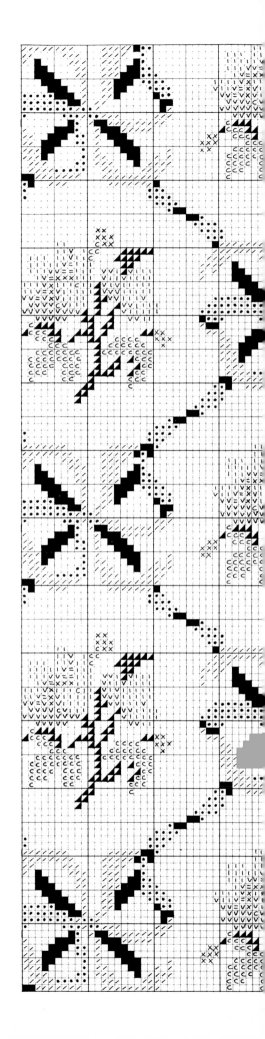 7768 green	
• 7798 sky blue		7853 pink
C 7548 pale green	✕ 7727 pale yellow	
V 7851 salmon pink	╱ 7800 pale blue	
■ 7797 medium royal blue	═ 7850 lobster pink	

36

Victorian floral pattern

• 7759 mulberry	☒ 7295 air force blue
☐ 7746 cream	‖ 7268 grape
⊘ 7367 green	

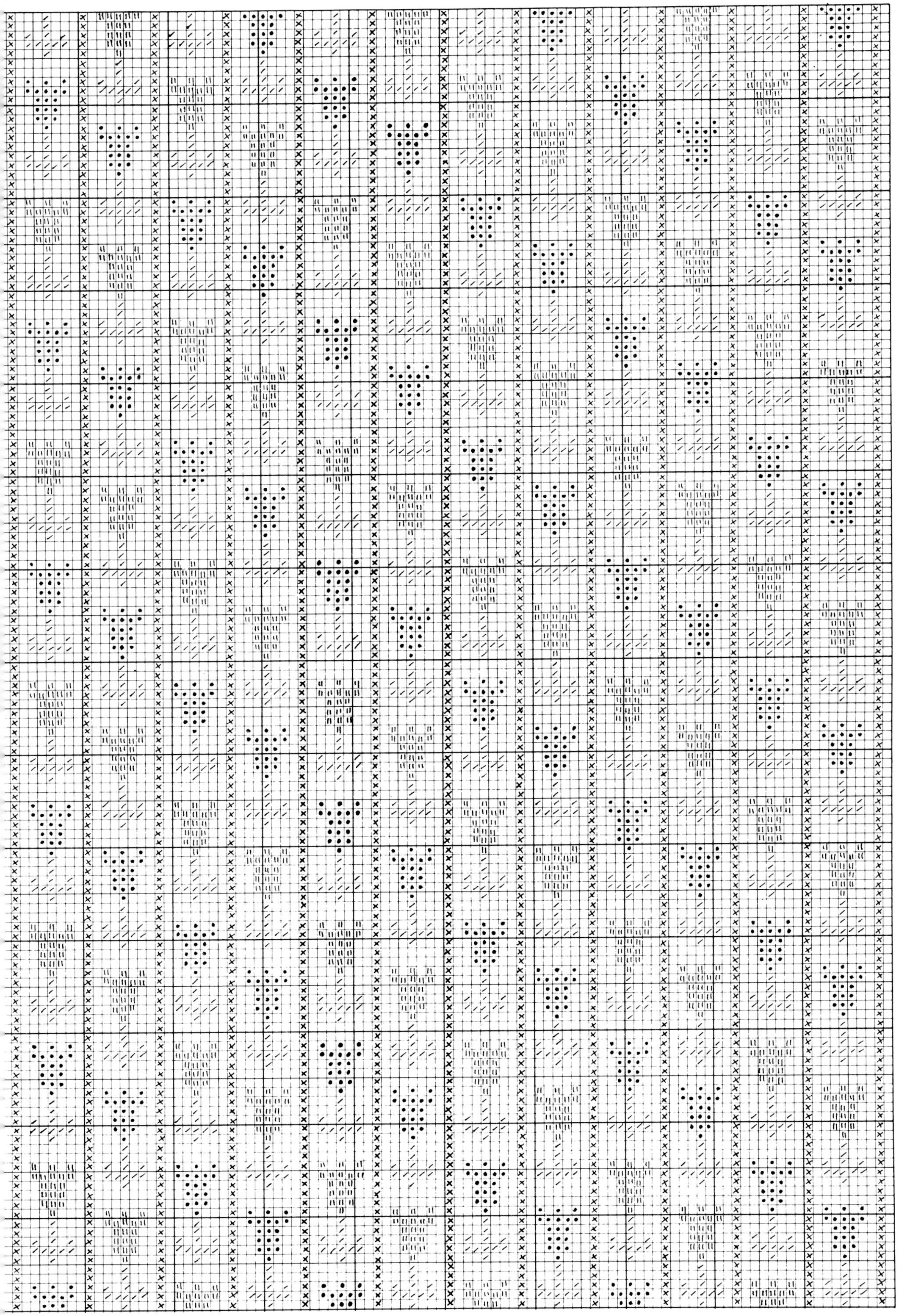

10

37

Grape vine

■ 7259 dark grape		□ 7251 pale grape	
□ black		‖ 7255 grape	
• 7424 light pistachio green		╱ 7427 dark green	

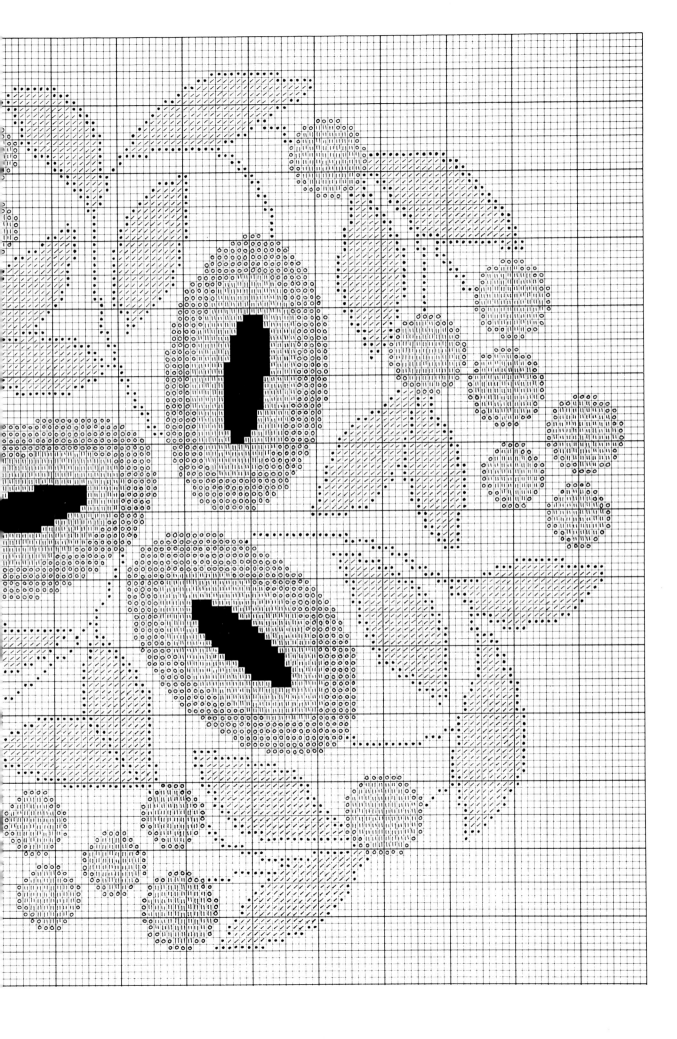

38

Dog rose

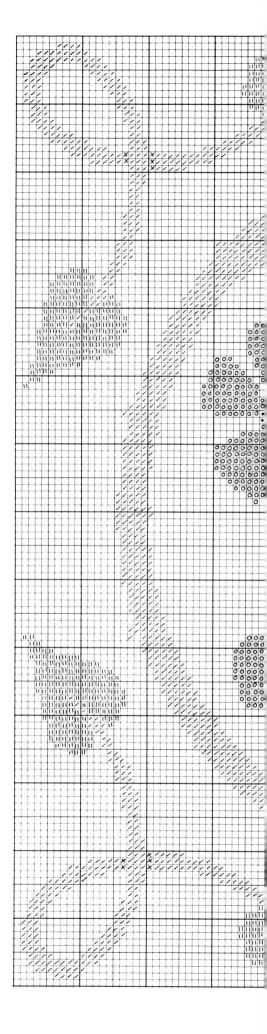

☐ 7288 dark air force blue	● 7745 pale yellow
⬦ 7845 brown	○ 7852 pink
☒ 7840 chocolate	‖ 7770 bright green

39

Pink tulips (1)

□ 7727 pale yellow   ☒ 7600 dark rose pink

⟋ 7605 rose pink   • 7768 green

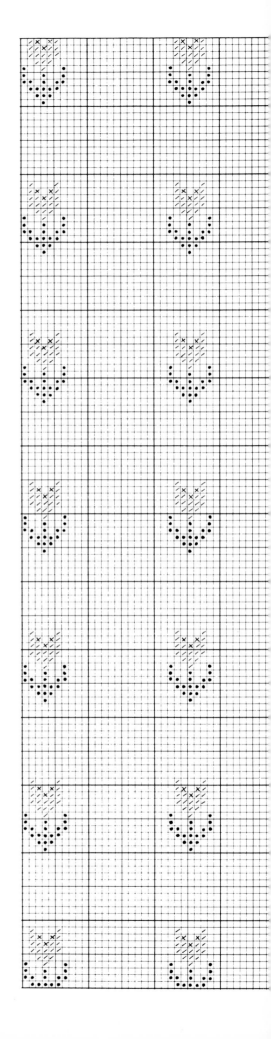

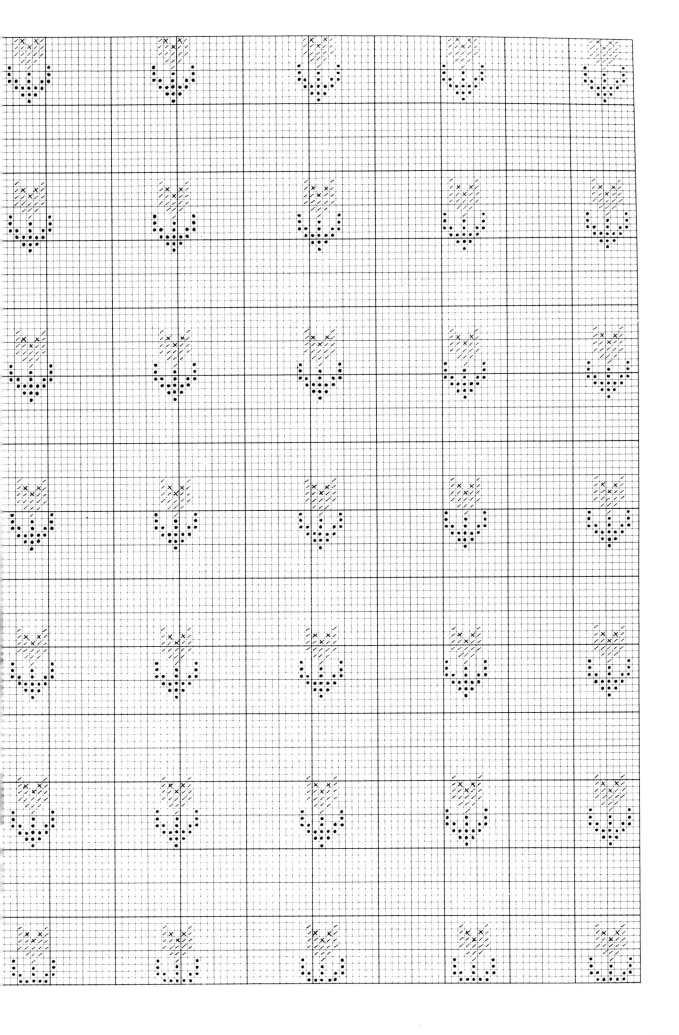

Pink tulips (2)

☐ 7727 pale yellow   ☒ 7600 dark rose pink

▨ 7605 rose pink   ⊡ 7768 green

Photo on p.114

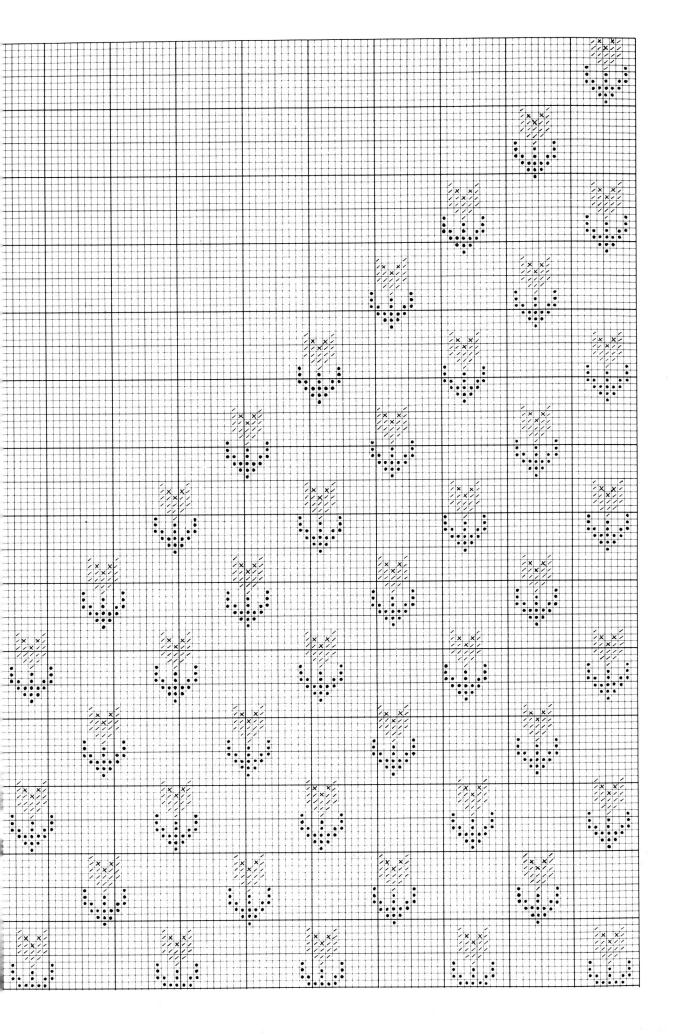

Pink
tulips
(3)

☐	7727 pale yellow	⊠	7600 dark rose pink
⊘	7605 rose pink	⊡	7768 green

Photo on p.115

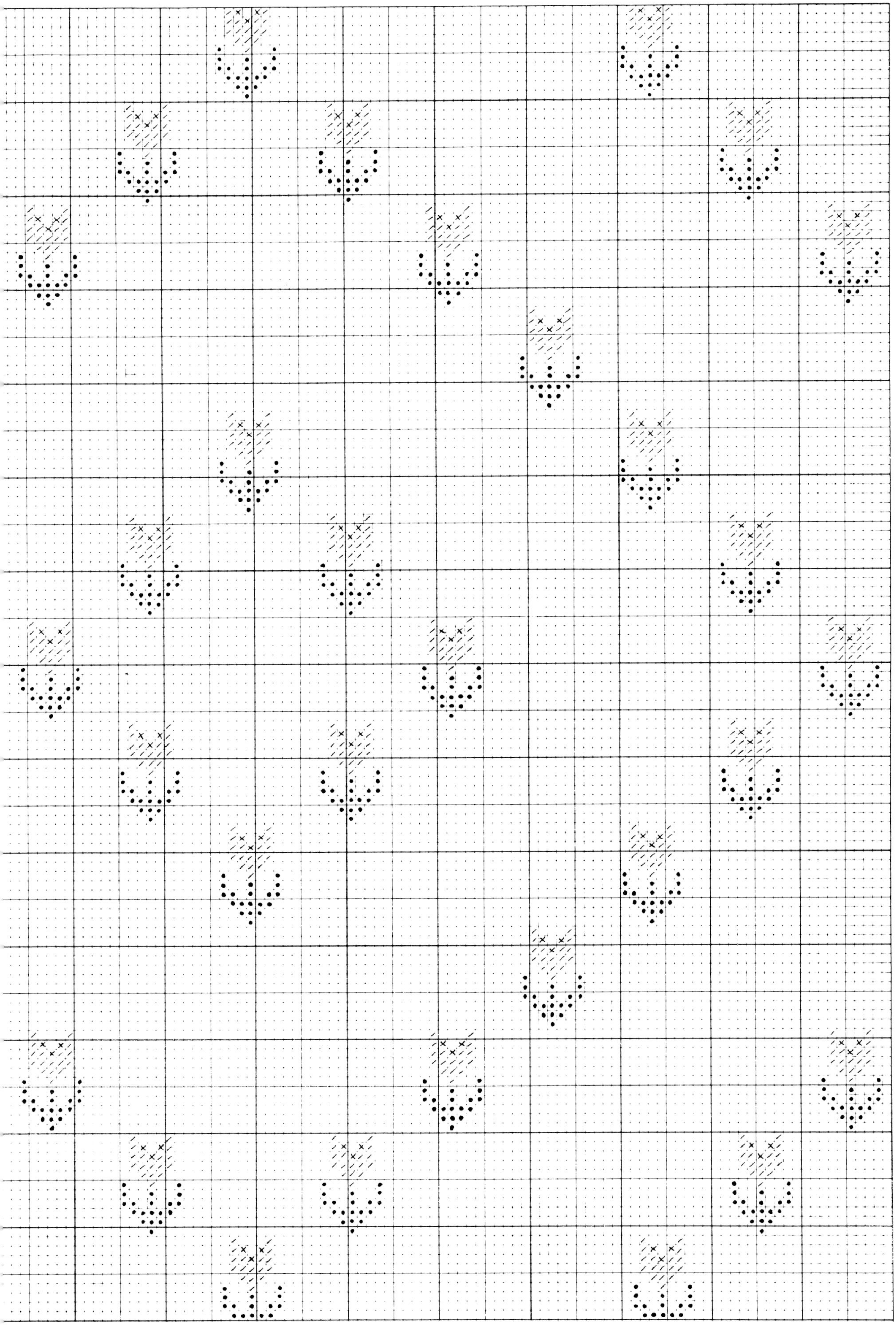

Pink tulips (4)

☐ 7727 pale yellow	☒ 7600 dark rose pink
⧄ 7605 rose pink	⦁ 7768 green

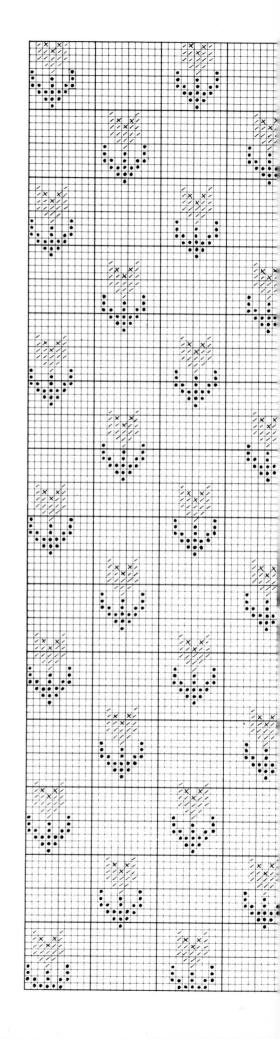

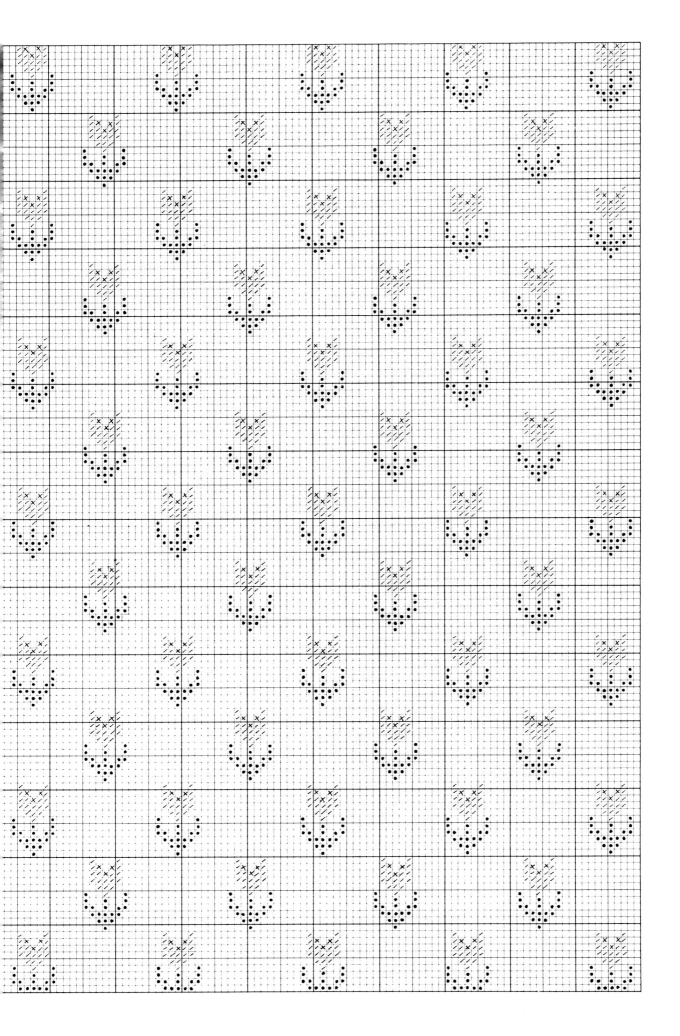

Pink tulips (2)
See p.108

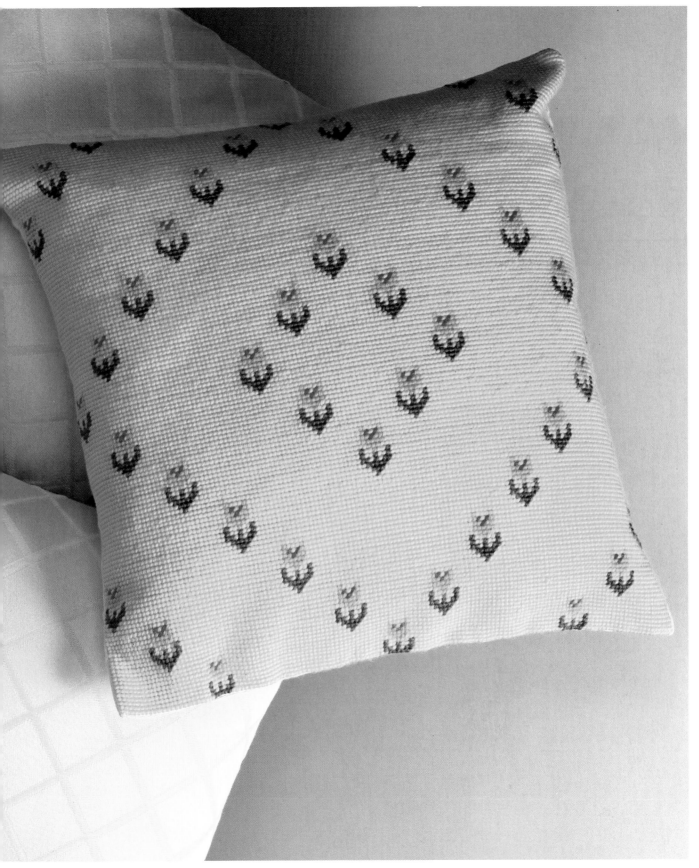

Pink tulips (3)

See p.110

Sunflower

■ 7950 dusky pink

□ 7801 dark brown

☑ 7786 yellow

Ⅲ 7782 dark mustard

• 7890 dark green

Ⓒ 7547 green

⬚ 7549 pale green

Photo on p.118

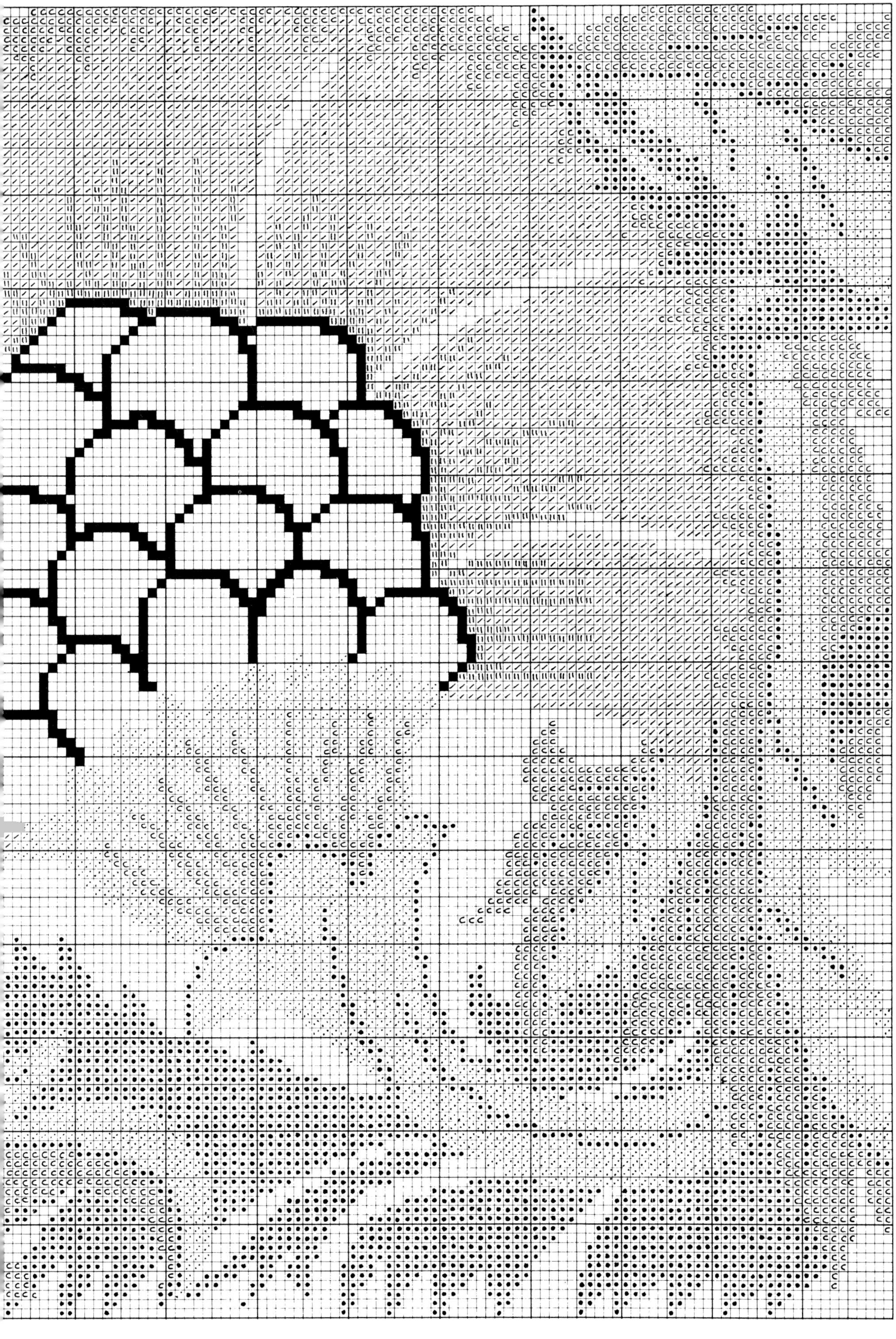

Sunflower

See p.116

44

Petals

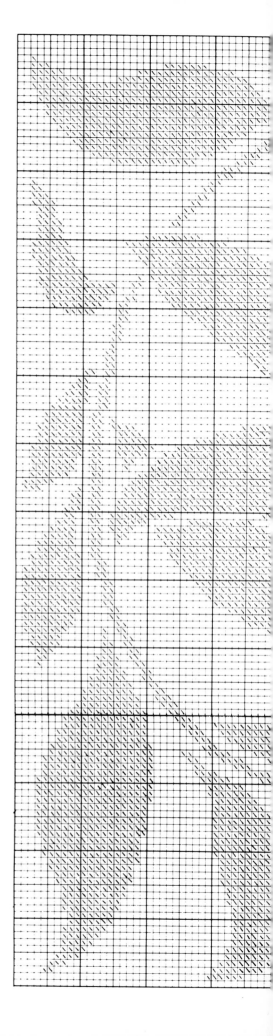

☐ 7930 dark air force blue

☑ 7604 pale blue/green

Photo on p.122

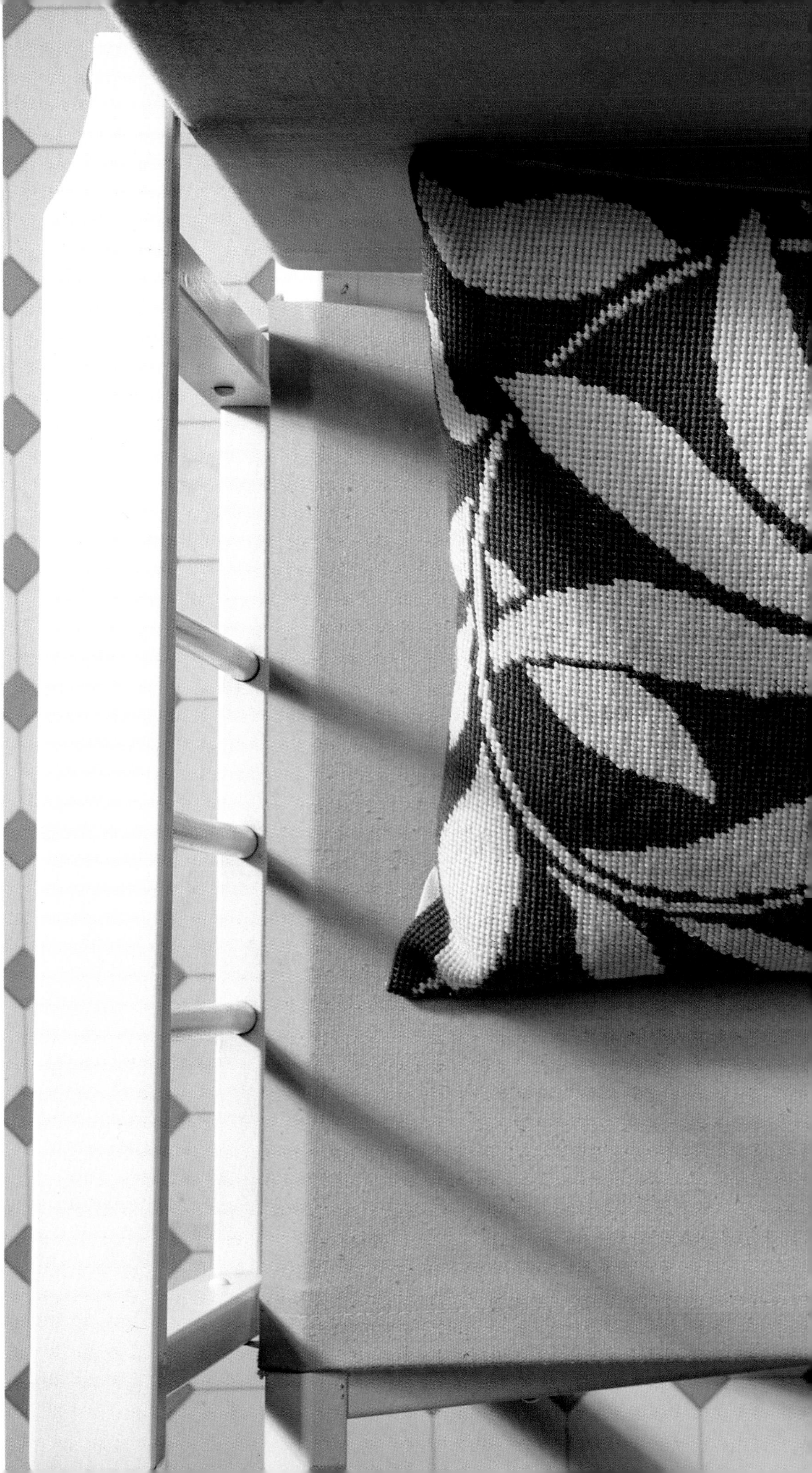

Petals
See p. 120

45

Raspberries

	black		7911 green
■	7840 chocolate	C	7715 pale grey
╱	7153 raspberry pink	•	7620 medium grey
‖	7846 tan		

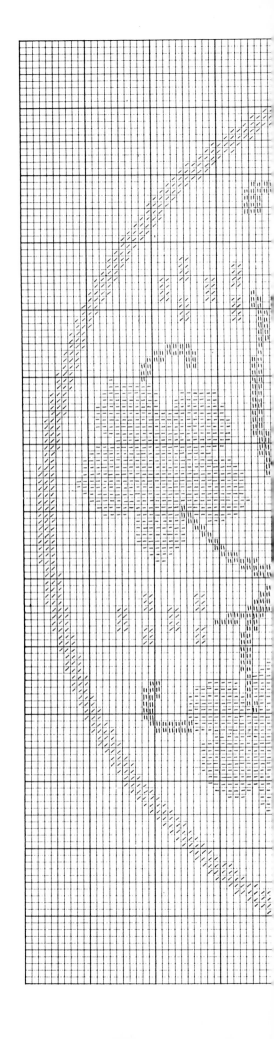

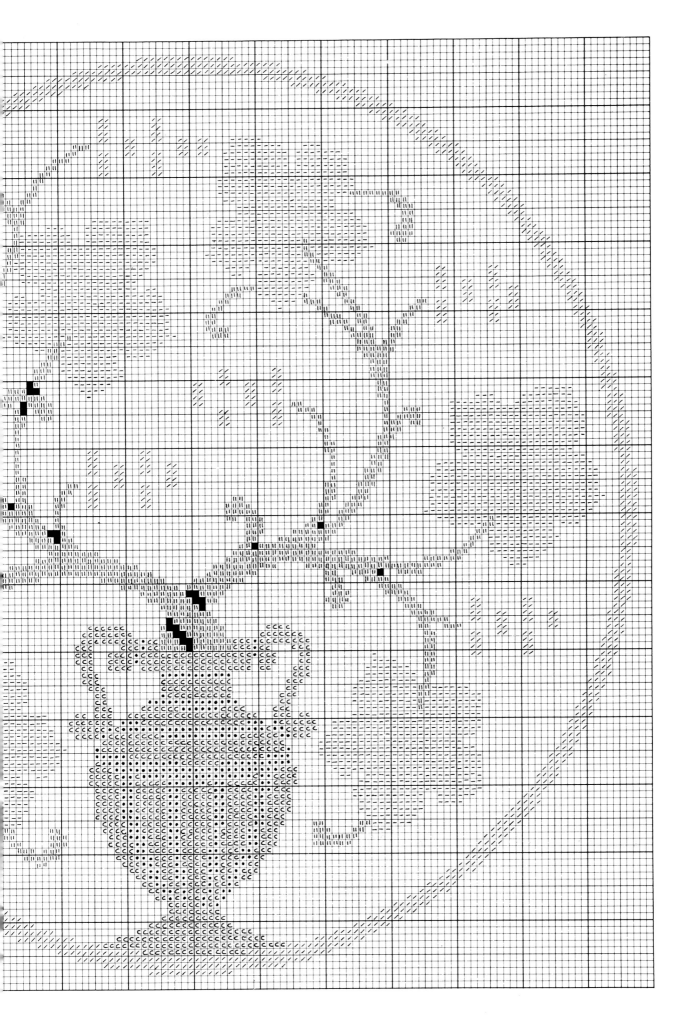

46

Exotic
flowers

■ 7259 dark grape		☒ 7251 pale grape	
☐ 7431 citrus yellow		⬙ 7257 medium grape	
• 7389 dark green		⊟ 7253 light grape	
⧄ 7344 green		‖ 7255 grape